Defending the North

The Fortifications of Ulster 1796–1956

Bill Clements

COLOURPOINT

To the Officers and Men
of the Antrim Artillery
1854 – 1956
and in memory of Liz

6 5 4 3 2 1

© Bill Clements
    2003

Designed by Colourpoint Books, Newtownards
Printed by The Universities Press (Belfast) Ltd

ISBN 1 904242 07 3

Colourpoint Books
Unit D5, Ards Business Centre
Jubilee Road
Newtownards
County Down
Northern Ireland
BT23 4YH
Tel: 028 91820505
Fax: 028 91821900
E-mail: info@colourpoint.co.uk
Web-site: www.colourpoint.co.uk

About the Author

Bill Clements was born and educated in Northern
Ireland, studying Law at The Queen's University of
Belfast. In 1958 he was commissioned into the 6th
Battalion The Royal Ulster Rifles (TA) and subsequently
became a regular soldier serving with The Royal Ulster
Rifles and then The Royal Irish Rangers. His interest in
fortifications began during a posting to the School of
Infantry at Hythe in Kent where he developed an interest
in the Martello towers. Later he was stationed in Gibraltar
and in 1969 he attended the Australian Staff College at
Fort Queenscliff, a Victorian coast defence fort near
Melbourne. He commanded the 1st Battalion The Royal
Irish Rangers and later served in the Ministry of Defence
in London, in Nigeria, Hong Kong and as Military and
Defence Attache at the British Embassies in Rangoon and
Peking, retiring from the Army in 1992. He is a member
of the Fortress Study Group and his first book *Towers of
Strength – Martello Towers Worldwide* was published in
1999. He now lives in London with two Korat cats.

Cover illustrations

Front cover:
Painting of manning the guns at Grey Point Fort in the
closing months of 1939.

Norman Whitla

Back cover, top:
Searchlight in its emplacement in the old fort at Dunree.

Author

Back cover, bottom:
Carrickfergus Castle. Although essentially medieval, the castle
and its fortifications continued to be developed until well
into the nineteenth century.

Norman Johnston

CONTENTS

Acknowledgements 4

Glossary 5

Preface 7

Introduction 11

1 The Board of Ordnance and the Defence Committees 17

2 War with France, 1798–1809 20

3 Lough Swilly, 1810–1815 26

4 Lough Foyle and Belfast Lough, 1810–1816 34

5 The Irish Signal Towers 39

6 The Years of Peace, 1816–1854 42

7 Fear of France and the Technological Revolution, 1855–1880 45

8 Breech-Loaders and Battleships, 1881–1900 53

9 The Approach of War, 1900–1914 62

10 World War One, 1914–1918 69

11 Between the Wars, 1919–1939 76

12 World War Two – Part One, 1939–1941 86

13 World War Two – Part Two, 1942–1945 96

Epilogue 103

Appendices 107

Notes 111

Bibliography 113

Index 114

ACKNOWLEDGEMENTS

Although I have known and visited the forts and batteries of Lough Swilly, Lough Foyle and Belfast Lough since I was a young boy, it was only in the last few years that I decided to relate their long and honourable history. When I started my research it quickly became apparent how little I actually knew about them but I was extremely fortunate to receive an enormous amount of assistance from a large number of people, to many of whom I was quite unknown until I approached them. I can only thank them for so willingly helping a complete stranger.

In Northern Ireland my thanks must go to Colonel WRH Charley who was instrumental in putting me in touch with so many people who had knowledge of Grey Point and Kilroot forts. Amongst these were Colonel BD Cotton, the last commanding officer of 429th Coast Regiment RA (TA) and Major The Earl of Romney who had served in 525th Coast Regiment RA during World War Two. My thanks also go to Brigadier IN Osborne, Secretary of the Northern Ireland Reserve Forces and Cadet Association, for helping me obtain access to the records of the Antrim Artillery; to Lieutenant Colonel J Hassett, the former Chairman of the Grey Point Fort Committee, for information on the refurbishment of the fort; and to Major HJF Potter, Chairman of the Northern Ireland in World War II Museum in Belfast. I must also acknowledge the kindness of Mrs Valerie Pounder for allowing me, on a wild and stormy autumn day, to tramp all around and photograph her lovely house which has been splendidly converted from a gun position.

South of the border I am indebted to many who went out of their way to help me. In particular, Colonel Declan O'Carroll of the Irish Army who, in 1986, wrote a short history of Fort Dunree. Colonel O'Carroll searched his records and notes to provide me with information and Commandant V Laing of the Military Archives in Dublin was equally assiduous in producing papers and records relating to Fort Dunree and Fort Lenan. Mr Paul Doyle, the Town Clerk of Buncrana Urban District Council, and Councillor J Sheridan are also due my thanks for providing access to Ned's Point Fort and Fort Dunree.

My thanks also go to a number of organisations without whose help my research would not have got very far. In particular, I am grateful to the staff of the Public Record Office in London, Derry City Council Heritage and Museum Service, the Northern Ireland Department of the Environment Heritage Service and Thales Optronics, the last-named being the latest incarnation of that famous old British company Barr & Stroud Ltd. I would also like to acknowledge the help I received from Mr Nicholas Hall, Keeper of Artillery at the Royal Armouries Fort Nelson. I am especially grateful to Bernard Meehan, Keeper of the Manuscripts at Trinity College Library and to Grainne MacLochlainn of the National Library of Ireland for so kindly waiving the reproduction fees for the use of numerous photographs and prints from their collections which I have used to illustrate this book. Finally, I have to thank Michael Pugh for providing the maps in the book.

Every effort has been made to obtain permission to use the pictures which appear as illustrations in the book. If I have failed to obtain permission in a particular case the fault is mine alone and I would ask the owner of the copyright to accept my sincere apologies.

GLOSSARY

amusette	long-barrelled, small-calibre wall gun
ashlar	square-hewn blocks of stone
ATS	Auxiliary Territorial Service
banquette	a raised walkway or step behind a parapet to enable troops to fire their weapons over the parapet
barbette	position in which guns are mounted to fire over a parapet wall rather than through embrasures in the wall
bastion	a defence work projecting outwards from the main walls of a defended place
batter	backward slope of the surface of a wall
BEF	British Expeditionary Force
BL	breech-loading
BOP	battery observation post
Bn	Battalion
breastwork	a fieldwork thrown up breast-high for defence
caponier	covered passage constructed across, or projecting into, a ditch to provide sheltered communication across the ditch or to defend it
chase	the portion of a gun barrel from the trunnions forward to the muzzle
carronade	large-calibre, short-barrelled gun
CASL	coast artillery search light (term used post-1940)
cavalier	a raised platform built on a bastion or curtain wall, designed to mount artillery and to command the surrounding ground
counterscarp	outer wall or slope of a ditch
curtain	main wall of a fortified place which runs between the towers, bastions or gates

DEL	defensive electric light (term used pre-1940 for a searchlight)
DEMS	defensively equipped merchant ships
embrasure	opening in a parapet or wall through which a gun can be fired
GHQ	general headquarters
glacis	open slope extending from the ditch giving a clear field of fire to the defenders
GOC	general officer commanding
gorge	rear, whether open or closed, of any defensive work
grillage	heavy framework of cross-timbering as foundation for building in treacherous soil
HAA	heavy anti-aircraft
holdfast	a steel plate secured into the ground by long vertical bolts sunk into a concrete base on which heavy guns in fixed positions were secured
HP	hydro-pneumatic
IRA	Irish Republican Army
keep	central tower of a fort or castle serving as a position of last defence
LAA	light anti-aircraft
lunette	a large outwork in the shape of a detached bastion
machicolation	gallery projecting from the wall of a tower with openings between the corbels through which fire can be brought on an enemy at the base of the tower
Martello tower	small circular tower, usually on the coast to prevent hostile landing
monitor	shallow-draught warship armed with heavy guns
MTB	motor torpedo boat
OC	officer commanding

palisade	a series of wooden or iron posts with sharp pointed tips used as a fence	SR	Supplementary Reserve
parapet	stone breastwork designed to give defenders on a wall or tower protection from enemy fire and observation	scarp	inner wall or slope of a ditch
		TA	Territorial Army
		terreplein	area on top of a rampart or tower and surrounded by a parapet where guns are mounted
pdr	pounder	tete de pont	fortification defending the approach to a bridge
QF	quick-firer		
RA	Royal Artillery	traverse	a defensive barrier, usually a wall or earth bank, placed at right-angles to the main line of defence in order to protect the defenders from flanking fire
racer	circular or semi-circular horizontal metal rail along which the traversing platform of a heavy gun moved		
RBL	rifled breech-loading		
RE	Royal Engineers	USC	Ulster Special Constabulary
redoubt	a small fortified work usually designed as an infantry stronghold	UVF	Ulster Volunteer Force
		wallpiece	small, muzzle-loading gun usually mounted on the wall of a fortress and traversed by means of a swivel (sometimes called a swivel gun)
RGA	Royal Garrison Artillery		
RIC	Royal Irish Constabulary		
RML	rifled muzzle-loading		
RUC	Royal Ulster Constabulary	ward	an outwork of a castle
SB	smooth- bore		

PREFACE

The coastline of the historic province of Ulster stretches from the mouth of the River Erne in the west, where it enters the Atlantic in Donegal Bay at Ballyshannon, northwards to Killybegs, past the almost vertical Slieve League cliffs and then along the north-western and northern shores of County Donegal. It continues through Londonderry and Antrim and finally ends in the glorious beaches of Tyrella Strand and Dundrum Bay at the foot of the Mountains of Mourne in County Down in the east. The indented coastline of Donegal is backed by inhospitable country with no major centre of population, presenting a potential invader with the problem of having to strike deep inland before attaining any major strategic objective. The north coast is penetrated by two major sea loughs, Lough Swilly and Lough Foyle, which provide access to the city of Londonderry, while Belfast Lough in the east leads to the ancient town of Carrickfergus and the city of Belfast itself.

Carrickfergus is the oldest of the three towns and its settlement dates from the thirteenth century when the Norman castle dominating Belfast Lough was built. Londonderry and Belfast were originally Plantation towns, the former established in 1600 by Sir Henry Docwra and the latter soon after by the Chichester family. By 1795 Belfast was developing faster than the other two towns, becoming an industrial city and overtaking Londonderry whose commerce remained based on a rural economy.

Lough Swilly is the longest of the three loughs, approximately 18 miles (28 km) in length. It is deep and has a good anchorage off the small village of Rathmullen and opposite Inch, some 12 miles (19 km) from the entrance between Fanad Head and Dunaff Head. Lough Foyle, just across the Inishowen Peninsula, east of Lough Swilly, leads directly to Londonderry. Shorter than Lough Swilly, it is 14 miles (22 km) from the entrance to the lough to the mouth of the River Foyle which is navigable for a further four miles (7 km) to the city itself. Lough Foyle is much wider than Lough Swilly but not as deep – shipping has to keep to a central channel which narrows to just over a mile wide (1.6 km) at the entrance between Magilligan Point in County Londonderry and the village of

Greencastle in Donegal. From a naval point of view, Lough Swilly provides a better anchorage for a fleet and was to be used as such by the Royal Navy early in World War One.

Belfast Lough is 12 miles (19 km) long, about seven miles (11 km) wide at the entrance and four miles (7 km) wide at Carrickfergus. It provided and continues to provide the main access to Ulster for commercial shipping. In the eighteenth century Carrickfergus was one of the principal towns of Ulster but lost its pre-eminence in the nineteenth century as Belfast became a large and prosperous industrial city, rivalling many of the largest cities in England. Its industrial strength lay in shipbuilding, engineering and weaving linen and by the 1850s it was the main industrial centre in Ireland.

Two other smaller loughs are to be found on the east coast of Ulster: Strangford Lough and Carlingford Lough. The former was considered too shallow and its entrance too narrow to be a viable approach for an invader, despite the proximity of the head of the lough to Belfast. Carlingford Lough provided access by water to the towns of Newry and Dundalk but was also an unlikely enemy objective since the entrance to the lough would require the enemy fleet to penetrate deep into the confined waters of the Irish Sea which, in the nineteenth and twentieth centuries, were firmly controlled by the Royal Navy.

In the period covered by this book only four approaches to Ulster were considered important enough by the British military planners to warrant permanent defences. These approaches were the three large sea loughs, Lough Swilly, Lough Foyle and Belfast Lough, together with the River Erne where it flowed from the western end of Lower Lough Erne to the sea at Ballyshannon. Upper and Lower Lough Erne together provided a barrier nearly 40 miles (64 km) long against an enemy force approaching Ulster from the west while the town of Enniskillen guarded the short stretch of land between the two loughs.

In the Revolutionary and Napoleonic Wars with France and in World War Two the threat to Ulster came from a European continent almost totally occupied by the enemy. The enemy invasion fleets could be launched from the French west coast ports sailing round Ushant and up the

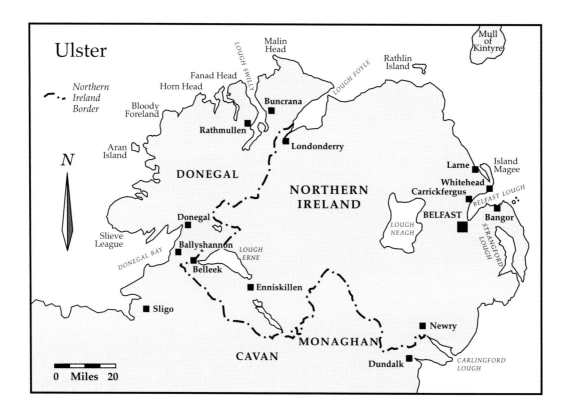

west coast of Ireland, or from the Netherlands or Denmark sailing up through the North Sea and around Scotland. In World War One invasion of Ireland was considered most unlikely, but the advent of submarine warfare brought a new threat which enhanced the importance of these deep sea loughs in Ulster as fleet anchorages and convoy assembly areas.

Despite the importance of the loughs, very little attempt had been made to fortify them prior to the Revolutionary War with France at the end of the eighteenth century. Defence of Belfast Lough depended entirely upon the guns of Carrickfergus Castle, mostly 18-pdr SB guns, with a maximum range of 1750 yards (1615 metres). As the castle was situated at a point on the shore where the lough was almost four miles (6.4 km) wide, the guns could do little more than cover the anchoring ground immediately offshore and, probably for this reason, by the middle of the eighteenth century the walls of the castle had been allowed to fall into disrepair.

The major fortification in the vicinity of Lough Foyle was the walled city of Londonderry itself. In 1790 the walls were still in reasonable condition but some of the gates needed replacing and there were no guns on the bastions, these having been removed some years before on the orders of the Board of Ordnance. The only fortification actually constructed for defence against shipping using the lough was the small triangular earthwork fort at Culmore Point at the mouth of the River Foyle some four miles (6.4 km) from Londonderry itself. The fort was built in 1600 enclosing the old castle, and in 1689 was captured by the Irish and French forces under James II. Its guns were used against the city during the famous siege but subsequently Culmore, having been used as a barracks, was allowed to fall into disuse.

No fortifications were provided for the defence of Lough Swilly before 1790 though the Ordnance Survey Memoir of 1834 reported and illustrated the remains of an old stone tower beside the ferry at Rathmullen, known as Fort Stewart. The Memoir writer, Lieutenant William Lancey RE, reported that "I have no information respecting it." Ballyshannon and the River Erne were also devoid of defences although there was a small military barracks at Ballyshannon dating from the beginning of the century.

The unrest in Ireland in the late 1790s and the threat of invasion by the French in this period and in the early 1800s forced the British military authorities to take steps to defend Ulster against seaborne invasion. This book is the story of the forts built at this time, their subsequent decline into obsolescence and their replacement by modern twentieth-century fortifications armed with rifled, breech-loading guns. These were the forts that provided the first line of defence against Hitler in World War Two, only finally to become obsolete when faced with attack by supersonic jet aircraft and guided missiles

Carrickfergus Castle: this Norman fortification has guarded the approaches to Carrickfergus and Belfast since the thirteenth century.
Author

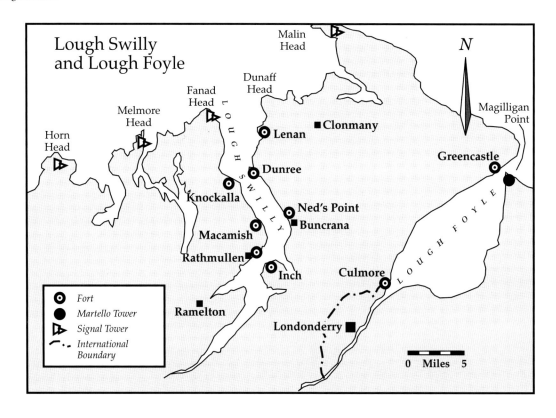

Lough Swilly and Lough Foyle

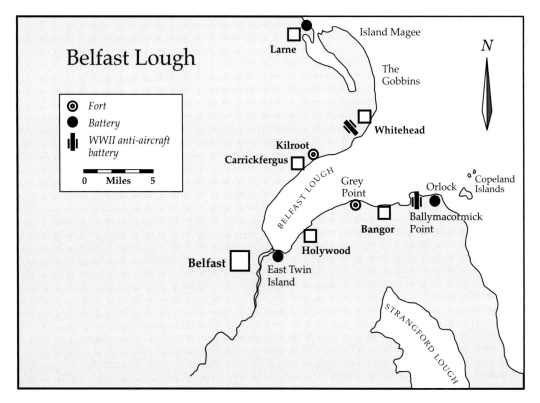

Belfast Lough

INTRODUCTION

Throughout the centuries since Strongbow's invasion of Ireland in 1170, the English have regarded Ireland as a turbulent land. For 300 years their control of Ireland was limited to an area around Dublin known as 'The Pale' and it was not until Henry VIII came to the throne in 1509 that effective efforts were made to bring all of the country under English control. These efforts came to a head under Elizabeth I and English jurisdiction was established in Connaught and Munster, but not in Ulster. Under Hugh O'Neill, Earl of Tyrone, Ulster was the last outpost of the Irish chiefs and it was here that opposition to English rule was strongest.

In 1558 Mary Tudor died and Henry of Valois, King of France, immediately recognised Mary, Queen of Scots, as queen of England, Scotland and Ireland, bringing an immediate threat of invasion to those parts of Ireland held by Elizabeth's forces. Ulster was particularly vulnerable to invasion by the Scots and although nothing came of the threat, in the eyes of Elizabeth's advisers it served to confirm what they most feared, that Ireland was a dagger pointing at the heart of England.

The threat from Scotland and France was soon followed by a much more serious threat from Spain. For over 20 years Philip II had been urged to invade England by English Catholic exiles, and Drake's action against Cadiz, together with the Earl of Leicester's support for the rebellious Netherlands with an English army were, in Spanish eyes, adequate grounds for an attack on England. However, it was the execution of Mary Queen of Scots that acted as the final spur that goaded Philip into action and the despatch of the Armada against England in 1588.

Until the Armada entered the English Channel, Elizabeth and her advisers were uncertain as to whether the Spanish objective was England or Ireland. Adverse weather contributed to the defeat of the Spanish as much as the actions of Drake, Hawkins and Frobisher. Nor were the further Spanish expeditions in 1596 and 1597 any more successful, though they continued to fuel the fears in English minds that a successful invasion of Ireland was always a strong possibility.

In 1598 open war broke out in Ulster and an English force of 3,000 men was defeated by O'Neill at the Battle of the Yellow Ford. This was the last major success for Hugh O'Neill and his allies. English reinforcements were dispatched to Ireland and for the next five years the Irish fought a series of rearguard actions against the new lord deputy, Lord Mountjoy, and his troops. In 1601 the Spanish attempted to intervene in support of O'Neill, this time successfully landing a force of 3,500 men at Kinsale in County Cork, probably as far from O'Neill and his forces in Ulster as it would be possible to get in Ireland. O'Neill marched south to join the Spanish and the combined force was defeated at the Battle of Kinsale. This was the first foreign invasion of Ireland since the arrival of Strongbow and, even though the Spanish force was defeated, it only served to confirm English fears about the vulnerability of Ireland to invasion by an enemy of England.

War raged across Ireland during most of the seventeenth century and in 1689 King James II, having been forced to flee from England by King William III and Queen Mary, landed at Kinsale with a body of French troops. The unsuccessful siege of Londonderry was followed by defeat at the Battle of the Boyne in the following year, resulting in James hastening back to France with the remnants of his supporters and their French allies. It was not until the middle of the eighteenth century that the next invasion of Ireland by foreign troops took place.

In the Seven Years' War from 1756 to 1763, England was in conflict with France and Spain. In 1759 the French prepared three expeditions against south-east England and the west coast of Scotland. The smallest of these three forces was that under the command of the French Commodore Thurot with seven frigates, a cutter and 1,100 troops. Of the three expeditions only Thurot's had any success and entered Belfast Lough on 21 February 1760. The garrison of Carrickfergus Castle, the only fortification protecting Carrickfergus and Belfast, comprised four weak companies of the 62nd Regiment. After bravely defending the castle, despite a breach more than 50 feet wide in the flank wall, until all ammunition had been expended including, according to some sources, the buttons on their uniforms, the garrison surrendered. Thurot remained in Belfast Lough for six days and then sailed on 27 February only to be defeated by a British force of three frigates on the following day.

Thirty years later, in 1793, Ireland was in a very disturbed state when war broke out again with France. The success of the American colonists in their War of Independence with England and the even more recent French Revolution had brought about calls in Ireland for the reform of parliament, restoration of civil rights to Catholics and even demands for an independent republican Ireland. These demands crossed all religious divides in the island and found supporters amongst Catholics, Presbyterians and even some Anglicans, all of whom felt aggrieved in their own way at the manner in which the English administered Ireland.

Two years earlier, in 1791, a group of Irish radicals had founded a secret committee to further their ideals for an independent Ireland. Initially called the Irish Brotherhood, it soon came to be called the Society of United Irishmen, a name coined by a young Dublin barrister who was to become the most famous United Irishman of all, Wolfe Tone. The United Irishmen quickly gained recruits to their cause and, initially, their main support came from a group of radical Presbyterians in Belfast, but they were soon joined by other Protestants and some Catholics in Dublin.

It was not surprising, perhaps, that with the coming of war with France in 1793 the United Irishmen were regarded as a dangerous revolutionary element which might be exploited by the French. Trouble in Ireland could only be to the advantage of the French since any civil unrest would tie down large numbers of English troops. On that basis Pitt's government took steps to suppress the Society of United Irishmen and other similar radical societies. Prosecutions of United Irishmen caused the movement to go underground and Wolfe Tone, who was known to have had contacts with the French, only escaped imprisonment by agreeing to emigrate to America. However, his sojourn across the Atlantic was a short one and he soon returned to Europe, quickly making his way to Paris seeking to persuade the French to support the United Irishmen and plan an invasion of Ireland.

With numerous sea loughs, wide bays and sandy beaches, most of the Irish coastline lay wide open to invasion. The proximity of the east coast and Dublin to England enabled the Royal Navy to protect these areas by preventing an enemy entering the Irish Sea through the narrow St George's Channel to the south or the even narrower North Channel between Fair Head and the Mull of Kintyre. Along the rest of the Irish coast it was a different matter, with all of it vulnerable to an attack by enemy invasion forces sailing from the French ports of Cherbourg, Brest or L'Orient, or from the Dutch ports and sailing around the north of Scotland.

Feasible as both approaches were, the French authorities gave a less than enthusiastic reception to Tone's plans. They were fully occupied beating off the assaults of the allied armies that were determined to crush the upstart revolutionary government of the Directory. Gradually, however, the Allies were forced back from the French frontiers, withdrawing from the Austrian Netherlands (Belgium) and Holland only to permit the occupation of these countries by the French and the foundation of the pro-French Batavian Republic. In Italy a French army led by the young Napoleon Bonaparte swept all before it, occupying Lombardy and the Papal States and bringing about the fall of the Venetian republic.

By the summer of 1796 the idea of spreading republicanism to Ireland and embarrassing the English government now appeared more attractive to the Directory and they listened more attentively to the United Irishmen who described persuasively a nation waiting to rise in opposition to a hated occupying power just as soon as a French force landed.

The Directory assembled a force of 15,000 troops under the command of General Hoche who was fresh from quelling the Vendeean uprising. The troops were to be carried in a fleet of 17 ships of the line, 13 frigates and corvettes together with transports all under the flag of Admiral Morard de Galles. The invasion force sailed for Ireland on 16 December 1796.

Misfortune dogged the fleet from the moment it sailed from Brest, with a collision involving the flagship *Fraternite* as the ships weighed anchor and the loss of the *Seduisant* (74) on the Pointe de Raz. The flagship with Hoche and the admiral became separated from the main body of the fleet and, failing to rejoin the fleet, returned alone to France. Meanwhile the bulk of the invasion force, having been becalmed in a dense fog for two days, successfully eluded the British fleet and arrived off Bere Island in Bantry Bay on the south-west coast of Ireland on 22 December.

They had arrived just too late because the weather changed and a strong easterly wind, which soon became a blizzard, prevented the French ships from making their way further into the bay and effecting a landing. Unknown to General Grouchy, Hoche's second in command upon whom the military command of the expedition had devolved with the disappearance of the flagship, the town of Bantry was almost defenceless. Only a small force of poorly trained Yeomanry under the command of the local landowner, Richard White, was mustered to oppose them.

The French made no attempt to land, sending only a single ship's boat and crew on a reconnaissance to Bere Island. The storm worsened and the new flagship was forced far out into the Atlantic, losing all contact with the rest of the fleet. With no lessening in the strength or direction of the wind by 27 December all the French ships had been forced out of Bantry Bay with no alternative but to return to France. The most serious French attempt ever to invade either Britain or Ireland had come to nothing.

In November 1796 Lord Carhampton, the newly appointed Commander-in-Chief of the forces in Ireland, travelled north on a tour of inspection. He was most alarmed at the state of the country as he found it and wrote to Chief Secretary Pelham saying that "it was in a much worse condition and more up to rebellion and nearer to start into action than you imagine should an enemy fleet land before the well-affected are collected and armed, and are aroused from their torpor and horror"[1]

The enemy fleet had failed to make a landing in Bantry Bay but their very presence was enough to throw the English authorities into a panic and encourage the disaffected United Irishmen. In March 1797 the government struck quickly and effectively. Under powers conferred by the Insurrection Act, which had been passed at the beginning of the previous year, General Lake, the commander of the Northern District, imposed what amounted to martial law on large parts of the north of Ireland. Ulster was disarmed and numerous suspect revolutionaries were imprisoned, the military acting on occasions with considerable brutality.

Despite the setback in Ulster, the Society of United Irishmen contrived to expand and by late 1797 there was a membership approaching 100,000. That summer most of the country was in a ferment and Ulster, in particular, was near rebellion. Rumours of a French invasion abounded but, despite all the efforts of the leaders of the United Irishmen to bring this about, the French government remained sceptical about the prospects for a successful Irish rising.

Sceptical as the French might be, they were not averse to encouraging the English government to believe that an invasion of Ireland might indeed be mounted – and quite soon. The more English troops that were deployed to defend Ireland the better as far as the French were concerned. Throughout the summer overt preparations were made to mount an expedition using the troops and ships of their new ally, the Batavian Republic, but, before a final decision to sail for Ireland could be made, the Dutch fleet was defeated by the Royal Navy at the Battle of Camperdown in October. To Wolfe Tone's disappointment there was to be no further attempt to mount an expedition to Ireland until the winter gales eased and the spring of 1798 brought better weather.

The 1798 Rebellion

Although Ulster had been largely disarmed and was under strict military control the other provinces – Leinster, Munster and Connaught – had been spared the rigours of the Insurgency Act. Lord Edward Fitzgerald was the most flamboyant leader of the United Irishmen who now numbered over 150,000 in these three provinces alone, many with rudimentary arms such as pikes and swords, with a small number of muskets and pistols. The question in February 1798 was whether to rise against English rule now or wait for the long-expected French expeditionary force.

In March an informer advised the authorities that a meeting of the Leinster provincial committee of the United Irishmen was to be held. This committee included members of the Super National Directory and on 12 March, 15 members of the Directory were arrested. Lord Edward Fitzgerald was not amongst their number but maintained his freedom for only a few weeks more before he too was arrested. The arrest of the leaders threw the United Irishmen into disarray and destroyed the coordination vital to a successful revolt. It is somewhat ironic that as the rebellion broke out, patchily and at half-cock generally, the French at last took the decision to send another invasion force against Ireland.

In January 1798 Bonaparte, on his return from Italy, accepted the command of the Army of England tasked by the Directory with the invasion of that country. Doubtful from the start that an invasion could be successful without French command of the sea, he carried out a tour of inspection of his army stationed on the Channel coast. Determined already to go to Egypt if the possibility of a successful invasion of England appeared in any way doubtful, Bonaparte quickly convinced himself that this was indeed the case. Advising the Directory that "we must really give up the expedition against England, be satisfied with keeping up the pretence of it",[2] he speedily converted the Army of England into the Army of the East and set off to capture the gateway to India.

The main rising of the United Irishmen in 1798 was around the town of Wexford, on the east coast 70 miles south of Dublin, with further outbreaks in Ulster around Antrim and Downpatrick. There was no coordination and the rebellion in Wexford was ended at the Battle of Vinegar Hill on 21 June, while the Ulster rebels had been crushed some ten days earlier. Yet it was only after the defeat of the rebels in Ireland that the decision was taken to despatch the French expedition, in reality a number of separate small expeditions. The largest force of 3,000 men under the command of Commodore Bompard and General Hardy was to sail from Brest, while a smaller expedition of 1,000 troops under General Humbert sailed from Rochfort. Another force of 1,000 troops in three frigates and a corvette was planned to leave the Texel to reinforce General Hardy, while a single ship carrying military stores and a small number of troops left from Dunkirk. If the Irish revolt lacked coordination so did the French invasion force, with Humbert's smaller force sailing some six weeks ahead of Hardy's main body of ships and soldiers.

Humbert with three frigates and his 1,000 troops, together with additional military stores to arm any Irish rebels who might rally to his flag, sailed on 6 August. Evading the English blockade they arrived in the Bay of Killala in County Mayo on 22 August and quickly disembarked.

The Irish flocked to join Humbert and, initially, his force increased to over 6,000 as a result of arming 5,000 rebels with the muskets brought from France. Two days after landing, Humbert led his troops due south from Killala towards the small town of Ballina, leaving 200 French troops to garrison Killala. The garrison of Ballina fled at his approach, allowing Humbert time to pause briefly to reorganise his small army. Humbert reduced his force to a total of about 1,500, comprising 800 French and 700 selected Irish rebels, and then led it on an attack on Castlebar, the largest town in County Mayo.

Instead of advancing by the most direct route, Humbert led his force by a circuitous route to the west over difficult and poor roads. Outflanking the English position on the outskirts of the town the French swept into the centre. The English force, which numbered about 3,000 poorly trained Militia and Yeomanry under the recently arrived General Lake, scarcely stopped long enough to oppose them. After the first few volleys the English broke and fled towards Athlone. Humbert had won his first and only victory in what came to be known as 'The Castlebar Races'.

For six days Humbert and his troops held a defensive position at Castlebar but as Cornwallis and Lake with 8,000 men approached Castlebar, the French slipped away northwards towards Sligo. Having captured the town, Humbert hoped to hold it as a base while awaiting the arrival of General Hardy and the main body. However, he was forced eastwards after contact with a small body of English troops holding a blocking position on the road to Sligo.

Humbert mistakenly took this force to be part of the army of General Cornwallis and so moved south towards Granard in County Longford where he believed he would be joined by a large body of rebels. Alas for General Humbert the rising at Granard had already been crushed and Cornwallis cornered the French force at Ballinamuck on 8 September. After a token resistance Humbert and his French troops surrendered on favourable terms, leaving his Irish allies to be slaughtered in large numbers. Ironically, the corvette *Anacreon* with 200 reinforcements, a large supply of military stores and a number of Irish rebel officers aboard including Napper Tandy, had sailed from Dunkirk four days previously.

Out of contact with Humbert and with little or no idea where the first expedition had landed, the *Anacreon* made landfall on Rutland Island lying just off the coast of County Donegal between Aran Island and the fishing village of Burtonport. Tandy and the French commander, Roy, disembarked and distributed leaflets stating that the French had come to 'liberate' the Irish and encouraging them to join with the French against their English oppressors. The edge was taken off this call to arms by the fact that the majority of the local population had fled inland and those few remaining passed on the news of Humbert's defeat at Ballinamuck. Tandy and Roy had no option but to re-embark and sail away. The corvette took the northern route round Scotland to Hamburg where Tandy disembarked only to be extradited to England shortly after.

Commodore Bompard's expedition, despite being the largest fleet to attempt a landing in Ireland since the ill-fated expedition to Bantry Bay two years earlier, was even less successful than Napper Tandy's abortive effort. A single ship of the line, *Hoche* (74 guns) and eight frigates and corvettes under the command of Commodore Bompard sailed from Brest on 16 September with 3,000 troops under General Hardy and Wolfe Tone. On 12 October the French ships were intercepted by a Royal Navy squadron off Tory Island, on the coast of Donegal. The English squadron of three ships of the line and five frigates was commanded by Commodore Sir John Warren. After an engagement lasting four hours the *Hoche* struck to HMS *Robust* (74 guns) aided by HMS

Magnamime (44 guns). With the capture of the French flagship the frigates made off as best they could but six were subsequently captured. The *Hoche* was brought into Lough Swilly to repair the damage and was later bought into the Royal Navy and renamed HMS *Donegal*. More will be heard of her, or at least of her guns, in the next chapter.

The defeat of Commodore Bompard and the capture of General Hardy and his force brought to an end all French attempts to invade Ireland for the next few years. Napoleon would assemble a huge invasion force on the French Channel coast in 1801–02 and again in 1803–04 and as part of his invasion plan he again considered landing troops in Ireland. However, without command of the sea, which the French Navy never appeared likely to achieve even briefly, there was no likelihood of such an invasion achieving success and these plans were soon abandoned. Nevertheless, the mere threat of an invasion from the Continent was sufficient to ensure that the coastal fortifications of Ulster were maintained until the end of World War Two in 1945.

The French line-of-battleship *Hoche* being towed into Lough Swilly by the frigate HMS *Doris*.
National Maritime Museum, London

The Board of Ordnance and the Defence Committees

Before describing the defences of Ulster it is, perhaps, appropriate to consider in some detail the departments and committees within the British Army which were responsible for the construction of these defences. In the early nineteenth century all fortification construction was the responsibility of the Board of Ordnance under the direction of the Master General of the Ordnance. The Board was one of three departments subordinate to the Secretary of State for War and the Colonies (the other two were the old War Office, under the Secretary at War, and the field army under the Commander-in-Chief, whose headquarters was in the Horse Guards building in Whitehall).

In many ways the Board of Ordnance was similar in organisation to the Board of Admiralty, having both civilian and military members. The chairman of the Board was the Master General who was also a member of the Privy Council and, as such, was the government's principal military adviser. The third most senior soldier on the Board, after the Lieutenant General of the Ordnance, was the Inspector General of Fortifications, the senior engineer officer of the armed forces. He commanded three professional corps: the Royal Artillery, the Royal Engineers and, from 1813, the newly formed Royal Sappers and Miners.

The four principal civilian officers were the Surveyor General, the Storekeeper General, the Clerk of the Deliveries and the Clerk of the Ordnance. The two principal permanent civil servants were the Secretary to the Ordnance and the Chief Clerk to the Clerk of the Ordnance. It was the Master General and the Inspector General of Fortifications, assisted by the two civil servants, who made most decisions without any direct responsibility to other branches of the government. However, when necessary the Board and the Inspector General of Fortifications would be advised on the validity of proposals and on technical matters by a Committee of Engineers. Such a committee comprised two or more senior Royal Engineers officers and was assembled when required. Indeed such a committee was assembled in Ireland in 1805 and travelled widely,

visiting Cork, Duncannon, Lough Swilly and Lough Foyle, recommending appropriate defences for these four harbours.

Subordinate to the Board of Ordnance were a number of ancillary organisations, in particular a body of officers in every military district and colony known as the Respective Officers. In fact the Respective Officers were a miniature of the Board and comprised the local senior artillery and engineer officers together with the local surveyor, storekeeper and clerk. The Respective Officers were responsible for supervising the expenditure of Ordnance funds within their districts once these funds had been authorised by the Board in London and as a result wielded considerable power independently of the district commander. We shall hear more of the Respective Officers shortly!

In 1805 the Corps of Royal Engineers comprised only 121 officers and 37 surveyors and draftsmen, though by 1815 this total had doubled. In each military district or colony there was a commanding engineer responsible for the supervision of all Board of Ordnance works, usually with one or more officers to assist him. In 1804 the commanding engineer in Dublin was Lieutenant Colonel Benjamin Fisher with four captains and a subaltern to assist him. Six years later Fisher had been promoted to brigadier general and the officer establishment of his department had increased to seven captains and five subalterns.

The engineer officers in the districts were responsible for preparing a detailed financial estimate for any building or fortification to be constructed and this was submitted to the Board of Ordnance through the local commanding engineer. Work could not start until the authority to do so was received from the Board and this, in practice, could be a long time since the Board was notorious for the length of time it could take before authorising work to start. Once work commenced the local Respective Officers strictly monitored the letting of contracts and supervised the expenditure virtually to the last farthing.

Where major Ordnance Board works existed or where

such works were under construction, an Engineer Office was usually authorised by the Board of Ordnance and in 1810 such an office was established in Buncrana. The staff employed by the office comprised a clerk of works, an overseer, a carpenter, a thatcher, a labourer to assist the thatcher and seven other labourers.[1] They were involved, primarily, in the maintenance of existing Board of Ordnance works since all major construction work was placed in the hands of local contractors such as Mr Edgar of Buncrana.

Prior to 1810 the supervision of the Ordnance works and properties in the Lough Swilly area was the responsibility of an officer holding the appointment of Assistant Engineer. In 1798 this officer was Captain Sir William Smith Bt who was not a Royal Engineer officer but, in fact, had been originally commissioned into the Loyal Essex Fencible Infantry. When his regiment was serving in Ireland, Smith appears to have been detached for service with the Irish Engineers. It is uncertain what his technical qualifications were but his attachment to the Irish Engineers may well have resulted from the shortage of both Irish Engineers and Royal Engineers at that time. Prior to the Act of Union in 1801 supervision of Board of Ordnance works in Ireland was the responsibility of the Corps of Royal Engineers in Ireland, or the Irish Engineers as they were more commonly called, a corps with a total of only eight officers at that time.

Certainly Colonel Fisher had reservations about Smith's competence to supervise the construction of the later fortifications built on the shores of Lough Swilly and Foyle between 1810 and 1815. Writing on 30 April 1810, Fisher complained: "I am anxious to make some beginnings at Lough Swilly – and I have no one I can confide in to hand there, for although the Assistant Engineer is a valuable officer, I apprehend that he is not quite equal to so extensive a charge."[2]

Despite Fisher's doubts Smith remained at Lough Swilly but his position does appear to have been somewhat unusual and was questioned as late as 1 July 1814 when we find him soliciting the brevet rank of major. He had been promoted to captain in the Loyal Essex Fencible Infantry but it seems he was accepted as Assistant Engineer in the rank of lieutenant by the Board of Ordnance and only given the local rank of captain. The matter of brevet rank was submitted to the Master General of the Ordnance and in a letter to Lieutenant General Mann, the Inspector General of Fortifications, the secretary to the Master General, wrote:

His Lordship not perceiving the name of Sir W. Smith in the Army List wishes to ascertain the actual situation of that officer, observing that if his rank be general Army Rank unattached to any particular Corps, the question of his Brevet Promotion can only be submitted to the Commander-in-Chief for His Royal Highness' consideration and order.[3]

Sir William Smith received a final bureaucratic reply from the Master General saying "that the rank of captain which was granted to him in the month of March 1804 is merely local rank which would cease with the discontinuance of his services under the Board of Ordnance. His Lordship is sorry he cannot recommend him for the Brevet promotion he solicits".[4] Sir William must have accepted his somewhat irregular position since he eventually spent 33 years in the Lough Swilly area where he had been involved with the defences from the very beginning. He died, still serving, at the advanced age of 80 on 18 January 1831 and is buried in the Church of Ireland churchyard in Buncrana.

As previously remarked, the Board of Ordnance was not noted for the speed of its decision making.

Sir William Smith's grave (foreground) in Buncrana churchyard.
Author

Overwhelmed with proposals and estimates, the Master General and the Inspector General of Fortifications were loathe to delegate authority to the Respective Officers. Delays of years in the authorisation of important works of defence were not unknown and indeed were actually quite common. This dilatoriness on the part of the Board frequently led to the local military commanders authorising the construction of fortifications as 'field works' and financing the work from their own budgets. To this dilatoriness on the part of the Board could be added further delays resulting from poor communications, the time required to prepare detailed financial estimates, the scrutiny of these estimates, and the preparing and signing of contracts. When all this is taken into consideration it is perhaps surprising that the Board successfully completed so many projects, both large and small.

The Board of Ordnance was always subject to the jealous eyes of both the Cabinet and the Treasury. The Cabinet decided the level of Army expenditure while the Treasury supervised the Commissariat and both suspected the Board of Ordnance of waste and being a drain on the public purse. Although subject to much criticism, the Board had a champion in the Duke of Wellington and as long as he lived no changes in the organisation of the Board were possible. Wellington's death in 1852 coincided with a campaign against large military expenditures, particularly overseas. The responsibilities of the Board of Ordnance in the colonies ceased shortly after the Duke's death and the Board, under further attack by Lord Grey and other reformers, was abolished in 1855. It, together with the other military departments, was absorbed into the new war ministry but the post of Inspector General of Fortifications did, however, remain, and Field Marshal Sir John Burgoyne held this appointment for a period of 23 years from 1845 to 1868.

The demise of the Board of Ordnance in 1855 brought the Royal Artillery, the Royal Engineers and the Inspector General of Fortifications directly under the control of the Commander-in-Chief. In 1859 the Inspector General of Fortifications became directly responsible to the Secretary of State for War for the execution of all engineer works and in 1868 he took on the additional role of Inspector General of Engineers, but in this role he was responsible to the Commander-in-Chief. In 1870 the archaic situation whereby the Commander-in-Chief was answerable only to the sovereign was finally ended and in that year he was made subordinate to the government by royal order. As an indication of his changed position, the Commander-in-Chief's headquarters was moved from the Horse Guards and established in the War Office in Pall Mall. The reforming zeal of the then Secretary of State for War, Edward Cardwell, resulted in the reorganisation of the Commander-in-Chief's staff and a number of permanent committees were set up. One of these was the powerful Defence Committee under the presidency of the Commander-in-Chief himself, with the First Sea Lord, the Adjutant General, the Quartermaster General and the Inspector General of Artillery among its members.

The Defence Committee took over the decision-making on all aspects of fortification at home and overseas and it had a number of technical sub-committees to advise it. These included the Heavy Gun Committee which advised on the provision of heavy guns and the armament of forts and batteries. In 1884 the Heavy Gun Committee was superseded by the new Royal Artillery and Royal Engineers Works Committee which took over the role of advising the Defence Committee on all aspects of fortifications and their armament.

In 1885 a further committee had been set up to consider all matters concerning overseas fortification. This was the Colonial Defence Committee and was separate from the Defence Committee which changed its name in 1899 to the Joint Naval and Military Committee with the Under Secretary of State for War as president. Further changes occurred in 1903 when both committees were each placed under the presidency of a Cabinet minister. A year later, on the advice of the Esher Committee, the two committees were amalgamated to form the Imperial Defence Committee with the Prime Minister as ex-officio president.

At the same time the Esher Committee abolished the appointment of Inspector General of Fortifications and his work was divided among several branches of the War Office, with the policy on fortification transferred to the General Staff. The RA and RE Works Committee was also abolished in 1904 and it was not until six years later, in 1910, that the Home Ports Defence Committee was set up. This was a standing sub-committee of the Imperial Defence Committee charged with advising that committee on the measures to be taken to defend the naval and commercial ports of the United Kingdom. Subsequently this became the Joint Overseas and Home Defence Committee and this was the situation until the outbreak of war in 1939.

War with France 1798–1809

Lough Swilly and Lough Foyle

The arrival of the French fleet in Bantry Bay in December 1796 had forced the military authorities in Ireland to review their plans for the defence of the country against invasion. The Commander-in-Chief, the Earl of Carhampton, advised Lord Lieutenant Camden that "the General Officers commanding in the several Districts aided by the Engineers have been instructed to examine and report on such Positions as they would recommend to be taken to oppose the advance of an enemy should he land within these Districts".[1] In particular, attention was to be paid to the defence of Bantry Bay, where the French had recently attempted to land, and the district commander was to report how practicable it would be to construct batteries on Whiddy Island and Bere Island. Similar reports were required on the defence of other bays including Lough Swilly.

In Ulster, where most of the country was in a political ferment, it might have been expected that immediate steps would have been taken to provide defences against a French invasion, if not for the three main loughs then at least for Lough Swilly, the latter being a deep sea lough which could provide a safe anchorage for the largest fleet and which was situated in close proximity to Londonderry. A number of local landowners were very vocal on the subject of the defence of Ulster and in their attempts to spur the military authorities into taking some action.

One of the foremost landowners in the north-west of the country, Sir George Hill, proposed the immediate raising of a corps of Yeomanry for the defence of Lough Swilly and the construction of a new fortification on Culmore Point at the head of Lough Foyle. At about the same time Thomas Knox of Dungannon pointed out that Donegal Bay, Lough Swilly and Belfast Lough presented gateways to an invader and he suggested that a redoubt should be built at Magilligan Point at the entrance to Lough Foyle. None of these suggestions were acted upon by the military authorities and the only new fortification to be built, or rather rebuilt, in the area was a private one. The owner of

the sixteenth-century Doe Castle at the southernmost end of Sheephaven, Captain John Harte, rebuilt the castle in the late 1790s and constructed an earthwork ravelin for five 9-pdr SB guns on the side of the castle overlooking the estuary.

It was the arrival of Bompard's ships pursued by a British squadron off the entrance to Lough Swilly, that appears to have been the stimulus needed to bring about the fortification of the lough. It may be that work had already started on the defences as a result of Lord Carhampton's earlier directive but the means to arm the new batteries was suddenly at hand when Bompard's captured flagship, the *Hoche*, was towed into the lough to undergo temporary repairs. The military commander in Ulster, Major General the Earl of Cavan, quickly requested that the Ordnance Department purchase eight of the ship's 42-pdr SB guns together with ship's carriages. The purchase was authorised but a subsequent request from the earl for some heavy mortars was turned down by the Commander-in-Chief in Dublin, Lord Cornwallis.[2] The guns were sited in a number of batteries, the locations of which were chosen by Captain Sir William Smith, the

Doe Castle, Donegal: this sixteenth-century castle was refurbished in the late eighteenth century by its owner Captain CV Hart.
Author

Knockalla Fort: this sketch by Sir William Smith shows the fort in the early stages of its construction in 1799.

The Board of Trinity College Dublin

Assistant Engineer posted to Lough Swilly with specific responsibility for the temporary works in the area.

Smith's solution to the problem was to defend the entrance to the lough with two small forts while providing additional batteries further up the lough to deal with any ships which managed to pass through the entrance. Since the actual entrance between Dunaff and Fanad Heads was over four miles (6.4 km) wide this was too great a distance to be covered by even the heaviest and most powerful guns then in service. The lough narrowed to one and a half miles (2.5 km) between Saldanha Head on the western shore and Dunree Head on the eastern side, a little more than six miles (10 km) in from the entrance. Here was the logical position to site the forts, to be known as Dunree (or East) Fort and Knockalla (or West) Fort, where their guns could attempt to defend the narrow channel.

Commenced in 1798, by the following year both forts comprised a number of barrack buildings surrounded by a wall and at Dunree Fort the entrance was by means of a drawbridge. Both forts were sketched by Sir William Smith in 1799–1800 and in 1800 the armament of Dunree Fort was shown as five 18-pdr SB guns, two 9-pdr SB guns and two French 42-pdr SB guns on ship's carriages, these latter two acquired from the *Hoche*. In addition there were two 1-pdr wallguns or 'amusettes'. The armament of the Knockalla Fort was shown in the same report to be six 18-pdr SB guns.[3]

It has not been possible to trace the authority for the construction of the two forts. Suffice it to say that when Captain Smith sketched both forts, Knockalla Fort in 1799

and Dunree Fort in 1800, both were in an advanced state of construction. The sketch of the Dunree Fort shows two barrack buildings, a section of wall on the land side, and a bastion or low tower on the highest point of the small promontory on which the fort is built. No gateway is shown in the drawing but a further sketch does show a drawbridge under construction. Two guns are depicted on the low tower and these are covering the landward approach to the fort. The 1799 sketch of Knockalla Fort shows two barrack buildings, larger than those at Dunree, a substantial gun platform sited below the barrack buildings, and part of a surrounding wall with a large gap where the gateway was later to be constructed. In this sketch there was no sign of the tower that can be seen today.[4]

Smith was a practical engineer and a realist who accepted that while these two forts would probably prevent a single enemy ship from entering there would be considerable difficulty in stopping an enemy fleet. He planned to cope with this eventuality by siting six further batteries along the shores of the lough above the two entrance forts. On the western shore temporary batteries were sited at Macamish Point opposite the town of Buncrana and at Rathmullen, a village just south of Macamish Point. On the eastern side two batteries were sited at Buncrana, one north of the town at Ned's Point and the other to the south at Saltpan Hill. Two further batteries were built, one on the northern tip of Inch opposite Rathmullen, and the other at Fahan, close to Inch.

These batteries were armed with a further six 42-pdr SB

Saltpan Battery, Buncrana: this single-gun battery is typical of the temporary batteries sited in Lough Swilly between 1799 and 1810.   *The Board of Trinity College Dublin*

guns taken from the *Hoche*, but unlike the guns at the two forts these were each mounted on traversing platforms. A traversing platform consisted of two baulks of timber each about 16 feet (4.7 metres) long held together by three crosspieces with a pair of small iron wheels fitted under the front crosspiece, and a second pair mounted on two longer legs attached to the rear crosspiece. These longer rear legs had the effect of raising the rear of the platform to an angle of about 15 degrees. The front wheels ran on a curved metal track called a racer, the rear wheels mounted on a similar track but one with a larger radius, and both tracks were laid on flat stones. The whole platform moved on a metal pivot which, on occasions, was just the barrel of an unserviceable gun sunk into the ground to an appropriate depth. The gun itself was mounted on a garrison carriage, or in the case of the French 42-pdrs, on a ship carriage and the whole was mounted on the platform. Using this platform the gun could be easily trained to follow a slow moving target such as a ship and the raised angle of the platform served to reduce the recoil when the gun was fired.

The batteries at Macamish Point, Ned's Point, Down of Inch and Saltpan Hill were each armed with one 42-pdr SB while at Rathmullen there were two of these guns. In all the batteries except Macamish the guns were sited behind large parapets of sodwork and earth or sand at the rear of which there was a banquette of rough masonry. However, at Macamish the natural rock of the promontory on which the battery was sited was used as the parapet.

The Dunree and Knockalla forts each had a magazine for powder and ammunition and a grate or stove for heating shot but the temporary batteries were only provided with moveable wooden magazines which each held 36 rounds of ammunition made in French vellum cartridges and lacked grates to heat shot.[5] Ned's Point and

Macamish Point both had small guardhouses at the rear of each battery.

The Peace of Amiens was signed in March 1802 but the cessation of hostilities was to last little over a year. By May 1803 England was once more at war with France and again faced with the threat of invasion from across the Channel or through Ireland. Once again it was clear that Ireland would prove fertile ground for any French attempt to raise an insurrection. Indeed Robert Emmet, a young Protestant United Irishman who had been in France in 1801 endeavouring to persuade the French to mount another expedition against Ireland, returned to Dublin in 1802. Encouraged by the renewal of war in 1803, Emmet issued a proclamation in July calling for an uprising in Dublin against the English authorities. Although in theory well-planned, the rising went off at half-cock and in a farcical climax Emmet and his remaining small group of supporters attempted to assault Dublin Castle. However, the rising quickly degenerated into desultory rioting and the troublemakers were soon dispersed.

Late in 1802 the continuing unsettled state of the country and deteriorating relations with France had prompted the military authorities in Ireland to review the state of the country's defences. In January 1803 Colonel William Twiss RE, a senior Royal Engineers officer on the staff of Southern District in England, was sent to Ireland to report on the defences. Summarising the 'great points' to be considered, he gave as the final two the need to give protection to the north in proportion to its exposure and importance, and to examine what sort of security could be given to the extensive and important harbours of Bantry Bay and Lough Swilly.[6]

Twiss believed that Dunree and Knockalla forts sited as they were could not prevent an enemy ship from passing into the lough and, furthermore, they were so commanded by the ground behind each that they were vulnerable even to musketry fire. He recommended that both forts should be abandoned and a new, larger, fort built higher up Dunree Hill behind the existing fort. He also recommended that substantial sea batteries should be built on Inch and at Macamish Point, while at Buncrana he proposed the building of a large tower.[7]

By 1803, despite the continuing threat of invasion, the defences of Lough Swilly were beginning to fall into disrepair. In a report dated April 1803 Colonel Fisher, the commanding engineer in Dublin, reported to the Inspector General of Fortifications, Lieutenant General Morse, that "the Forts and Batteries on Lough Swilly remain nearly in the same state as they were during the last war".[8] Generally the guns were in good condition but at Dunree Fort the parapets, traverses and cavalier were reported as "contemptible" and the drawbridge unfinished, though the platform was serviceable. The remaining batteries were said to be in reasonable condition though at Ned's Point and Macamish the guard houses were in ruins and barely repairable. The Fahan battery, however, scarcely justified the title as it was a single 24-pdr SB gun mounted on a standing carriage on the ground without platform or parapet. However, the gun was said to be in good condition.

At the time of this report the garrisons were provided mainly by the Militia or the fencible infantry. At Dunree Fort the garrison comprised one acting Ordnance storekeeper and one bombardier and six gunners of the Royal Artillery together with what was described as an officer's party of the 79th Regiment. At Ned's Point there was a piquet guard of Yeomanry while at Saltpan Hill there was a sergeant's party of the 79th Regiment. Knockalla Fort had one lance bombardier and one gunner of the Royal Artillery and the Rathmullen Yeomanry garrisoned both the fort and also the battery at Rathmullen. Indeed at Rathmullen the report stated that "the Rathmullen Yeomanry are on Duty and have all of them been taught the Gun exercise".[9]

However, by October 1805 the situation at the batteries had deteriorated further. The Clerk of the Ordnance, on an inspection tour of the north of Ireland, reported:

> It is impossible, however, for any Common Observer to pass through the Batteries belonging to Lough Swilly without being struck by the disgraceful Manner in which they are constructed. As there is now a Committee of Engineers in Ireland acting under immediate Order of the Master General I beg leave to recommend it to the Board to request his Lordship to direct the Gentlemen to examine and report upon the State of the Works at Lough Swilly.[10]

The Committee of Engineers comprised Brigadier General Gother Mann RE (later to be Inspector General of Fortifications) and Lieutenant Colonel Robert D'Arcy and in August and September 1806 they inspected Lough Foyle and the fortifications along the shores of Lough Swilly. Their report was to result in a complete reconstruction of the defences of Lough Swilly and, for the first time, the fortification of Lough Foyle .

Belfast Lough

Despite its increasing importance as a commercial port throughout the eighteenth century, Belfast had never been strongly defended. Its main defence had always been its situation at the head of a long lough on the north-east coast of Ireland and close to Scotland and England. Its security depended on the Royal Navy, though the navy had failed to protect Carrickfergus in 1760 when Thurot attacked the castle and town with a small force of French troops. Then the castle, the only defensive fortress guarding the approach to Belfast, was in a ruinous state. Part of the curtain wall had collapsed and only after the defeat of Thurot were steps taken to improve the state of the castle's defences. However, despite the repair of the wall the castle remained essentially what it had always been, a medieval structure whose towers and walls had never been constructed to withstand artillery fire.

In 1793 Lieutenant Colonel Charles Tarrant of the Royal Irish Engineers had carried out some work to strengthen the castle. This work included strengthening the roofs of the two towers flanking the main gate to convert them into gun platforms. He also supervised improvements to the covered way that led from the main gate towards the town and this involved raising the walls and opening musket loops along their length.[11]

Eleven years later, in 1804, the armament of the castle was shown as being 14 12-pdr SB guns, two 6-pdr and six 4-pdr SB guns, all mounted on standing carriages and firing through embrasures. In addition there were three 'wallpieces'.[12] The use of standing carriages meant, however, that the guns were limited to engaging targets only when they came in line with the gun which, because of the difficulty in moving the carriage, was virtually fixed in the position it was pointing with only a small degree of elevation possible. In order to engage ships effectively guns needed to be mounted on traversing platforms and be positioned to fire en barbette.

Although Carrickfergus Castle remained the sole fortification on the shores of Belfast Lough, the Ordnance Survey map of 1835 showed battery positions at Macedon close to Belfast on the north shore of the lough and on the Ormeau demesne on the banks of the River Lagan, almost in the city itself. It is probable that

Carrickfergus Castle: this sketch made by Sir William Smith in 1800 shows the covered way on the left of the castle, one of the improvements made in 1793 by Colonel Tarrant.

The Board of Trinity College Dublin

these 'batteries' were probably the remains of earlier works or were temporary field works since none of the Ordnance Board returns of land and buildings of this period make any reference to either site.

Some thought was given in 1804 to improving the defences of Belfast with a proposal to construct two Martello towers on the shores of the lough. A list of Martello towers in Ireland made in that year mentions two towers in "Belfast Bay" but it appears nothing came of this proposal. Certainly there was no further mention of these towers in later lists of Irish fortifications and armaments and no remains of them can be found today.[13]

Lough Erne and Mid-Ulster

The main crossing points over the River Erne are at Ballyshannon, Belleek and Enniskillen. Ballyshannon, on the shores of Donegal Bay, has a good sandy beach two miles (3.2 km) west of the town which could be used by an invading force, while there is a bridge across the River Erne in the town itself. A small barracks was built at Ballyshannon as early as 1700 but by no stretch of the imagination could it be described as a defence work and the walls of the barracks were only designed to keep out 'ill-disposed persons'. The bridge itself, however, was protected by a form of defence which Sir William Smith described in his sketch in 1797 as a *tete-de-pont*. This work was much smaller than the later *tete-de-pont* at Shannonbridge in County Offaly. It took the form of a small stone redoubt sited on a hill on the west of the River Erne. The rear was protected by a semi-circular outwork with the main door in the side wall. There were two large embrasures in the redoubt wall overlooking the river which could clearly be used by artillery though there was no indication that any guns were permanently mounted in the redoubt. However, in 1803 there was reference to a half brigade of artillery being stationed at Ballyshannon and it is possible they were based in the defence work.[14]

A few miles up the river there was another bridge at Belleek, a small village which in the late eighteenth century was an important communications centre where roads linking Sligo, Donegal and Enniskillen met. Here too Smith constructed a redoubt on high ground overlooking the bridge. This was a larger work than that at Ballyshannon and, like the former, was also sited on the west of the river overlooking the bridge. The front of the work was a half-star in plan, comprising a central spur with the section of wall on each side angled forward forming a sort of demi-bastion where it met the flank walls. The upper section of the front and side walls was loopholed for musketry fire while at the front, below the

Belleek Fort, 1799 – sketch by Sir William Smith.   *The Board of Trinity College Dublin*

loopholes, there were eight embrasures for cannon. Inside the redoubt along the flank and rear walls there was accommodation for the garrison and storerooms while a semi-circular outwork, similar to the one at the rear of the Ballyshannon outwork, protected the entrance on the west side, furthest from the bridge.

It is of interest, and perhaps surprising, that the redoubt was sited to face an attack from the east rather than from the west. This suggests that when the redoubt was built the British authorities were more concerned with an internal threat rather than an external one and this is confirmed by a letter from Captain Smith, the assistant engineer who supervised the construction of the redoubt. In 1827, 29 years after it was completed, he wrote: "I received an order to lay out the covered embrasures so as in the darkest night to command all the fords on that water [River Erne], and they were so done as to command them completely during the rebellion of a dark night."[15] As long as the fort was held by the forces of the Crown the bridge could not be used by an enemy force. After Waterloo the redoubt had a much reduced military significance though it continued as a small barracks. Its moment in history was still to come.

In his report of 1803 Colonel Twiss recommended the construction of two large towers at Enniskillen on knolls which commanded the two bridges and where previously temporary redoubts had been built during the earlier war with revolutionary France. These towers were not built

but a permanent redoubt was constructed to act as the western defence for the town. Like the redoubt at Belleek it also was sited on high ground overlooking the bridge leading to the town. It was square in shape and surrounded by a glacis and a ditch, the latter 15 feet (4.6 metres) wide, and on each corner there was mounted a 5.5-inch (140-mm) iron howitzer on a traversing platform. This new redoubt and the larger bastioned earthwork fort dating from the seventeenth century Williamite Wars formed Enniskillen's main defences. In addition, the castle was modernised in 1796 at a cost of £7,000 and used as barrack accommodation for a battalion of infantry and adapted for local defence.

The only other fortification in central Ulster was the sixteenth-century fort at Charlemont in County Armagh on the Blackwater River close to the border with County Tyrone. This was a demi-bastioned fort originally built, together with a number of others, to control Ulster after the defeat of the O'Neill. Although garrisoned by English troops in the seventeenth and eighteenth centuries, at the beginning of the nineteenth century it was used only as a barracks and artillery store and as a defensive position had little military value. Colonel Twiss suggested the construction of a new fort in a location between the mouth of the Blackwater River where it enters Lough Neagh and Stewartstown on the southern shores of the lough but, once again, nothing was done by the military authorities to implement this proposal.

Lough Swilly
1810–1815

Improvement of the Lough Swilly defences was a long-drawn-out and tedious business. In 1806 the Committee of Engineers proposed to reform Dunree and Knockalla forts by increasing the capacity of each to mount ten guns and nine guns respectively. The temporary batteries at Macamish Point, Ned's Point, Rathmullen and Inch were each to have a tower mounting two guns and permanent batteries. At Ned's Point the battery was to mount four guns, Inch five guns, and Rathmullen five guns and two mortars. Macamish was to be a mortar battery mounting two large mortars.

For three years the plans were considered by the Commanding Engineer in Dublin and the Board of Ordnance in London. Even a report by a renegade French general did not produce immediate action. General Charles François Dumouriez, victor of Valmy, had arrived in England by a roundabout route after a failed attempt, in 1791, to re-establish the monarchy in France with Louis XVII as King. In 1803, shortly after Dumouriez had arrived in England, he was commissioned by the British government to write a report on the defence of England. In 1808 he prepared a further report, this time on the defence of Ireland.

In his report on Ireland, Dumouriez identified Lough Foyle, Lough Swilly and Belfast Lough as potential invasion routes. For Lough Foyle he recommended the construction of batteries at Magilligan Point, Greencastle, Redcastle, Whitecastle and Lower Moville and batteries on both sides of Lough Swilly together with a fort on the north point of Inch. However, despite these reports, no attempts were made to start work on improving the defences of the two loughs until 1809 when deteriorating relations between England and the United States and a rumour that Napoleon, now at the height of his power, was contemplating a new expedition against Ireland, added urgency to the Board's deliberations.

Despite the apparently urgent need to start work, a debate continued concerning various details of the design, particularly of the towers. In October 1809 the Board of Ordnance was considering a proposal to erect square towers at Knockalla Fort and Ned's Point but it was noted that a suggestion to surround each with a ditch would incur further expense.[1] Fisher was also unhappy with the design for the entrance into the tower on Inch, pointing out that "the side on which it is masked is the safest" and that "the loopholes devised in the tower by Colonel D'Arcy for the defence of the rear of the battery will be difficult to execute".[2]

It was an easy matter for the Board of Ordnance to order the work to commence on all these forts. It was quite another matter to get the work started on the ground. Captain Smith was unable to obtain tenders from local contractors for construction of the forts and batteries. In a letter to the Commanding Engineer in Dublin he complained: "I repeatedly made the most Public advertisements; resorted to putting up handbills, and in short, used every measure to give the fullest and fairest trial to the required mode of competition," but all to no avail.[3]

The problem was that there was a dearth of suitable contractors in the Donegal and Londonderry area who were competent to carry out the work to Board of Ordnance standards. Compounding this problem was the fact that the Respective Officers in Dublin would not authorise work to start until they had received competitive tenders. Smith continued:

> sundry proposers . . . did resort to me with crude proposals for the detached parts of the intended Works and had authority been vested in me, as formerly, on the spot, some contracts might have been made . . . but when it was explained that all proposals must be determined in Dublin, or elsewhere, these proposers made too many mortifying "reflections".[4]

This bureaucratic procrastination was actually part of a struggle between the Commanding Engineer and the Respective Officers. Previously considerable authority to accept tenders had been delegated to the Commanding Engineer and, on occasions, to the junior engineer officers on the spot. By 1809 the Commanding

Engineer, Colonel Fisher, was in dispute with his fellow Respective Officers. Fisher believed that the work could be completed much more quickly if the officers in the field retained authority to accept tenders locally. In a letter to the Inspector General of Fortifications dated 25 September 1810 he wrote:

If the Officers of the Corps of Engineers serving in Ireland, together with the direction, control and management of the Public Works, heretofore exercised by them are now to be placed under the command of the Respective Officers of Dublin, then in this case I must leave it to your better judgement to represent the matter in its true colour . . . I have no personal enmity or dislike to any of the Respective Officers, my difference with them, and the matter of which I complain, are founded first on the tardiness of the proceedings in respect of carrying on the King's Works, in the Engineers Department of which some services may be ordered by the Master General and the Board, two years before they can be begin upon. This may be exemplified in the case of some of the Coast Defences.[5]

According to Captain Smith at Buncrana the two local contractors, Mr Edgar and Mr Knowles, were both reluctant to tender for the Lough Swilly works. In the same letter quoted above Fisher went on to explain to Lieutenant General Morse that the Respective Officers required proposals for work to be carried out at Ned's Point and he believed it was impossible to get fair proposals and therefore saw no prospect of being able to carry out his order.

The outcome of this struggle between the Engineer Department and the Respective Officers in Ireland can no longer be traced. Whether the Respective Officers eventually received proposals that were to their satisfaction or whether they delegated authority to commence work without competitive tenders being received, we shall probably never know. Suffice to say Mr Edgar received the contracts to build or rebuild six of the forts and batteries on the shores of Lough Swilly.

However, further controversy was to arise when Colonel Fisher received a letter from a Mr John Bateman of Buncrana complaining about the poor design and construction of the Lough Swilly forts which he believed had wasted a large amount of public money and, in his letter, he implied that Captain Smith was lining his own pockets with the funds provided for the construction of the fortifications. Bateman scoffed at

the location of Dunree and Knockalla forts, maintaining that he could take both with 50 men and two 6-pdr guns. Bateman's mistake was to criticise a project which had already been authorised, after due consideration, by the Board of Ordnance. Fisher and the other Respective Officers in Dublin closed ranks and Captain Smith was given their full support and all suggestions that he was lining his pockets with Ordnance Board funds were rejected out of hand.[6]

A greater sense of urgency was introduced into the proceedings in 1811 when Napoleon once again appeared to consider invasion of either England or Ireland. In that year a force of 40,000 men was assembled in the Scheldt and it soon became known that the objective of this force was to be Ireland. In fact this was just a cover plan for a French attack on the West Indies.[7] Napoleon's attack on Russia in 1812 finally removed any threat of invasion but the government could not really rest easy for in the same year war broke out with the United States and there now existed a new threat of attack by American commerce raiders.

With the contracts let to Mr Edgar, in want of any other contractor willing to tender, work could proceed on the forts and batteries selected for improvement. In the case of Lough Swilly this meant all the existing forts and temporary batteries except the battery at Saltpan Hill and the single gun sited at Rinena Point near Fahan.

This was not likely to be an easy task. Colonel Fisher wrote to Lieutenant Colonel Rowley on 30 April 1810 acquainting him with some of the problems that faced him in Ireland, particularly in Lough Swilly. As always there was a shortage of Royal Engineer officers and Fisher wrote:

I am anxious to make some beginning at Lough Swilly . . . and I have no one I can confide in to hand there . . . indeed the station being so very far asunder, renders the superintendence of two or three officers necessary, for the Irish contractors are such a set, to which add the bitterness of people in office here.[8]

Later that year Fisher moved two additional engineer officers, Captain George Cardew and First Lieutenant Robert Power, to Lough Swilly to take over the supervision of the works from the inimitable Captain William Smith. Smith remained in his capacity as Extra, or Assistant, Engineer and the reconstruction of the forts and batteries started in 1811.

Dunree and Knockalla forts

In the rebuilding Dunree, or East, Fort retained its site on the small promontory jutting out from Dunree Head despite the fact that it was not an ideal location, being dominated by Dunree Hill, 335 feet (103 metres) high, to its rear. The fort is best described in the words of Lieutenant W Lancey RE who, in 1834, surveyed the area for the North East Donegal volume of the *Ordnance Survey Memoirs of Ireland*. Lancey described the fort as follows:

> The Fort occupies the whole of this peninsula and is inaccessible except by a drawbridge thrown over the chasm. It is an irregular 4-sided figure measuring 650 feet [200 metres] round the inside of the walls and parapets, and presents a fire of nine 24-pounders on traversing carriages, and three others can be mounted in embrasures if required.

> A ship entering the lough would have to contend with the direct fire of four guns. In passing by the fort she would also receive the direct fire of four others and after passing it the same number. The principal battery consists of six 24-pounders, four of which cross the fire of Knockalla [West Fort], one fires up, the others down the lough. Towards the entrance of Lough Swilly, and above the main battery, is a single gun, and immediately above it, on the most commanding part of the rock, two are mounted on a Martello tower which fire over the fort. The terreplein of the main battery is about 90 feet [27.69 metres] above the sea and that of the tower 35 feet [10.76 metres] above the battery.

> Dunree [East Fort] is commanded by musketry from an adjacent hill but the six gun battery is protected by buildings and the single gun battery by the tower the wall of which is raised towards the country to protect the gunners.[9]

From this description it is clear that the 18-pdr SB guns originally mounted in the battery had been replaced by the heavier 24-pdrs when the fort was rebuilt. The two 24-pdr SB guns on the Martello tower traversed using a single rear pivot which was a characteristic of the design of the Irish circular two-gun Martello towers. Behind the six guns in the main battery there was a furnace for heating shot.

According to a report of 1816 the fort had accommodation for two officers and 85 NCOs and other ranks.[10] However, by 1834 the garrison comprised a total of eight: a Master Gunner and seven gunners. The accommodation consisted of two slate-roofed stone buildings, a larger L-shaped one for the soldiers and a smaller, separate one for the two officers. These buildings were on the same level as the single gun battery, above the main battery but below the level of the tower. The rear wall of the fort was loopholed on either side of the gate and there were other loopholes above the gate itself. To the left of the gate as it was approached there was an oval-shaped bastion with loopholes which provided additional protection to the entrance.

The tower of the fort was not a typical Martello tower being, in fact, a raised platform for the two guns. Situated at the highest point on the small isthmus, the wall of the tower varied in height between 26 feet (8 metres) and 15 feet (4.6 metres) owing to the irregular lay of the ground. Internally there was no bomb-proof arch or central pillar to support it and it was approached up a long flight of steps leading directly to the parapet from the main fort rather than by the more usual ladder.

As Lieutenant Lancey pointed out in his 'Memoir', Dunree Fort was dominated by the hill behind it, and in 1805, before the decision to rebuild the fort had been taken, a plan had been submitted to the Inspector General of Fortifications for a tower mounting one gun on a traversing platform to be constructed on the summit of the hill. The tower was never built and until the end of the century the fort remained vulnerable to the fire of an enemy occupying the top of the hill.

Across the lough, Knockalla Fort was also rebuilt, retaining its earlier triangular form. The base of the triangle was formed by the parapet wall of the lower battery running along the edge of steep cliffs which fell directly to the sea. The other two sides were formed by the landward walls of the fort and where these met, at the apex of the triangle, a cam-shaped Martello tower was added. The fort was larger than Dunree Fort with the main, or lower, battery mounting seven guns on traversing platforms. The rebuilding of the fort enabled the number and type of guns that armed it to be reviewed. The opportunity was taken to concentrate at Knockalla Fort seven of the eight French 42-pdr SB guns taken from the *Hoche* which had previously armed the smaller temporary batteries around the lough and these were mounted on the lower battery. On the north end of the upper level of the fort there was a battery of two 24-pdr SB guns, also on traversing platforms, firing *en barbette* while on the Martello tower there were two 5.5-inch (140-mm) SB howitzers.

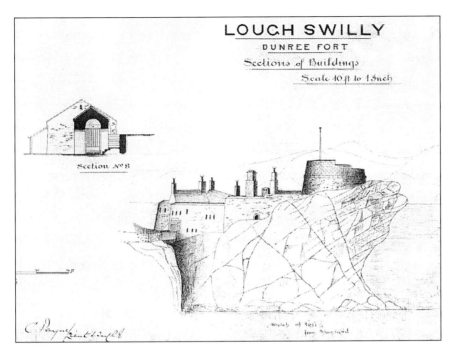

Left: Drawing of Dunree Fort: this sketch was made in 1893 but the fort had not changed materially since it had been re-built in 1812–1815.

PRO WO 78/4609

Below: Dunree Fort, County Donegal: a late nineteenth-century photograph from the Lawrence Collection.

National Library of Ireland

The Martello tower was similar in shape to the towers built on the east coast of England, being cam-shaped. At its widest it was 65 feet (20 metres) and about 30 feet (9.2 metres) high. Although this type of Martello tower normally mounted three guns on traversing platforms the tower of Knockalla Fort had mountings for only two and in place of the third there was a stone turret with a conical roof which provided access to the spiral staircase linking all the floors of the tower. It may well be that originally the tower did mount three guns as the existing tower is not the original one. Captain Sir William Smith and Mr Edgar seem to have been in dispute regarding the construction of the tower. Certainly there is a sketch made by Smith in 1815 showing the tower having collapsed and with a note at the bottom of the picture saying: "Sketch of the Tower at Knockalla Fort, made after the Fall thereof in order to show the infamous work made therein by the contractor, the fall having been foretold by Captain Wm. A.Smith Assistant Engineer prior to the same in 1815."[11]

The pivots of the gun mountings on the tower are of interest as they are of a pattern unique to Ireland. In the English Martello towers the pivot was often a condemned gun mounted vertically with the muzzle pointing upwards and with an iron spike projecting from it. In Ireland at this time, however, no condemned guns were available so the pivots had to be specially made. For Knockalla Fort these took the form of a single wrought iron spike supported by four concave wrought iron supports and similar pivots are to be found on the defensible guardhouse at Rathmullen.

The tower was rebuilt with a raised crenellation on the landward side of the parapet. Knockalla Fort, like Dunree Fort on the opposite side of the lough, was dominated by high ground behind and this raised crenellation was designed to protect the gunners from musketry fire from the hill.

Knockalla Fort from the landward side. *Author*

Within the fort there were quarters for the officers and barrack accommodation for the soldiers provided in a long L-shaped single-storey building on the upper level. Abutting the inside of the landward walls were further buildings including stores and a guard room beside the gate. Outside the walls was a ditch 20 feet (16.15 metres) wide and a low glacis. The approach to the fort was by way of a sunken road that cut through the glacis on the south side and led to an arched gateway. This gateway was flanked by loopholes in the wall on each side and the entrance was also defended by three more loopholes in the lower storey of the tower which enabled musketry fire to be brought to bear along the length of the ditch. Additional loopholes were provided at the base of the lower battery parapet wall where it met the upper level wall on the south side and where it was possible, although difficult, to approach the lower battery across the ditch.

According to the Ordnance Survey Memoir of 1834 the fort had accommodation for two companies of infantry and one of artillery, but for the whole of its history it is doubtful if the garrison ever exceeded the dozen or so men recorded as constituting its garrison in 1803.

Macamish and Ned's Point batteries

Along the western shore of Lough Swilly, 3.7 miles (5.9 km) south-east of Knockalla Fort (West Fort), a small promontory called Macamish Point juts into the lough. This was the site for a temporary battery of one 42-pdr SB gun which used the natural rock of the promontory as a parapet. This gun was replaced by a tower and a battery of three guns and once again the engineers made the maximum use of the natural rock to form a parapet

over which the three guns fired *en barbette*.

The decision to build the battery on Macamish Point resulted from the report of the Committee of Engineers which, in 1806, considered the defences of Lough Swilly. The role of the battery was to provide crossing fire with the new fort to be constructed at Ned's Point on the eastern shore, a mile (1.6 km) or so north of the small town of Buncrana.

Initially there was some indecision concerning the armament of the battery and tower. In a letter dated 26 July 1805, before the committee had considered the matter, Colonel Fisher suggested the construction of a battery on the point for three 24-pdr SB guns together with a single 8-inch (203-mm) SB howitzer mounted on the tower. The guns of the battery were to be sited so that one of the guns fired north up the lough while the other two fired east across the lough.[12] However, the committee under the direction of Major General Gother Mann RE did not support the proposal. Instead it suggested an armament of two guns for the tower and two 13-inch (303-mm) SB Land Service mortars for the battery. Mortars were considered a useful adjunct to guns in coast batteries because of the size of the explosive shell which they fired and the destructive effect such a shell had when it hit a wooden ship. The difficulty, however, was actually hitting the target as, with a long time of flight, they were ill-suited to engaging moving targets, even those that moved comparatively slowly.

Fisher's opinion ultimately won the day and the armament of the battery reverted to three 24-pdr SB guns and two further 24-pdr SB guns were mounted on the tower. The planned positions of the guns in the battery changed to two firing north up the lough and one firing east across it. The two guns on the tower were mounted using a single rear-mounted pivot which gave both guns almost a 360 degree traverse.

Entrance to the battery was by way of a drawbridge over a gully that ran between the isthmus and the mainland. Within the battery area there was a magazine built of rubble stone and another small stone building which was possibly a store. The tower was circular in shape with a door at first floor level entered by means of a ladder and above the door was a machicolation. In 1816 the battery and tower could accommodate two officers, three NCOs and 50 other ranks.

Immediately across the lough from Macamish Martello tower and battery was the fort at Ned's Point. Here the engineer officers responsible for the design decided against building a Martello tower and, instead, substituted what is referred to in contemporary documents as a "defensible guardhouse". This was a two-storey rectangular masonry building with musket loops at the basement and ground floor levels enabling fire to be brought against an enemy assaulting the rear of the fort or who had entered the dry ditch which protected the two landward sides.

It was Colonel Fisher who substituted the defensible guardhouse, or "quadrangular tower" as he called it, for the circular tower originally planned. Today it is not clear why he preferred the latter to a Martello tower. Possibly cost was a factor, since the rectangular building was probably cheaper to build, or it may have been a lack of skilled stonemasons. Certainly a number of these guardhouses were built elsewhere in Ireland at that time, notably at the mouth of the River Shannon and further up the river near Shannonbridge, so the design was familiar to the Royal Engineers officers of that time and, indeed, was unique to Ireland.

However, the Ned's Point guardhouse differed from those on the Shannon in that it was joined to the landward walls of the battery where these met at a right angle, whereas the Shannon guardhouses were free standing and surrounded on all four sides by a dry ditch. Unusually, at Ned's Point in addition to two loopholes in the lower section of the guardhouse, which enabled the ditch and main entrance to the fort to be covered by musket or rifle fire, there was also a large window. In the Shannon guardhouses this window was at ground level rather than level with the ditch so it is possible that the window in the Ned's Point guardhouse was inserted when the height of the building was reduced later in the century.

The battery and tower were completed in 1812 at

which date the armament comprised four 24-pdr SB guns on traversing platforms in the battery and two 5.5-inch (140-mm) SB howitzers on traversing platforms on the roof of the guardhouse and using separate pivots. The magazine held 80 barrels of gunpowder and at the rear of the guns there was a furnace for heating shot.

In 1816 the fort was described as having accommodation for two officers, four NCOs and 60 other ranks but in the same year the actual garrison was shown as three gunners, three NCOs and 20 soldiers from a line battalion.[13]

Rathmullen and Inch forts

The last two forts defending Lough Swilly were those at Rathmullen, a small town on the western shore of the lough, and on Inch south of Buncrana and immediately opposite Rathmullen at the narrowest part of the lough. Rathmullen was actually little more than a village and its sole claim to fame was that it was from Rathmullen that the O'Neill and the O'Donnell embarked for France in 1607 in what became known as 'The Flight of the Earls'. The *Ordnance Survey Memoirs of Ireland* described Rathmullen in 1834 thus: "It is about three furlongs in length and consists of a narrow, ill-built and dirty street of fishermen's houses and about half a dozen residences for persons of middling circumstances." However, its real importance as far as defence of the lough was concerned was that opposite the fort was the best anchorage in the lough in ten fathoms (18.5 metres) of water.

The new fort at Rathmullen was sited on the headland at the eastern end of the village abutting onto the beach. Constructed of squared rubble masonry it mounted five 24-pdr SB guns on traversing platforms and, like the fort at Ned's Point, instead of a Martello tower the design provided for a rectangular defensible guard house mounting

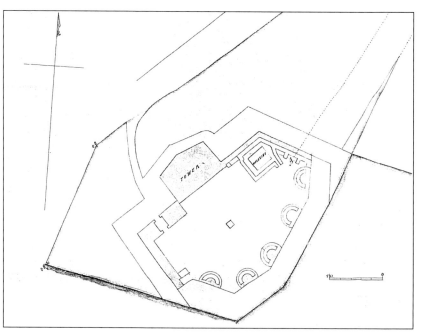

Plan of Rathmullen Fort.   *PRO WO 55/851*

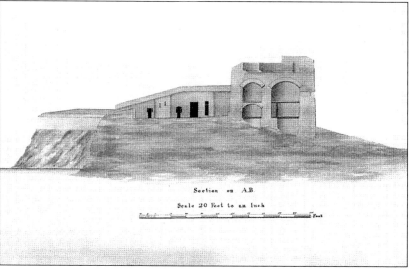

Section of Inch Fort.   *PRO MPHH 1/643*

two 5.5-inch (140-mm) SB howitzers. The guardhouse was located in the centre of the rear wall of the battery and its rear wall was angled outwards towards the centre, giving it a shallow D-shape rather than being straight, as was the rear wall of the guard house at Ned's Point.

The landward sides of the fort were defended by a ditch and glacis and the entrance was approached by a curved sunken road which led to an arched gateway flanked by a loopholes in the wall and in the lower level of the guard house. Inside the entrance and flanking it there was a small guard room built against the wall while in the north west corner of the battery there was a small magazine. There was a second magazine in the basement of the guardhouse and between them they held 220 barrels of powder. In the centre of the fort, behind the terreplein, there was a furnace for heating shot.

Across the lough and linking the fire of its guns with those of Rathmullen Fort there was a fort on the north-west tip of Inch. Known as Down of Inch Fort, it was larger than the one at Rathmullen both in area and number of guns; indeed in plan it was similar to the West Fort at Knockalla. The front scarp of the battery was irregular since it followed the natural line of the low cliff

on which it was sited and on the terreplein six 24-pdr SB guns were mounted. The battery was roughly triangular in shape with a cam-shaped tower securing the gorge. The two rear, or landward, walls were protected by a ditch and a low glacis and once again entrance was by means of a sunken road cut through the glacis and leading to an arched gateway as in the other forts. The tower was constructed of squared rubble masonry and was similar in shape to the English east coast Martello towers which mounted three guns. At Inch Fort these were 5.5-inch (140-mm) SB howitzers. An accommodation block and storerooms were built inside the fort along the landward walls and a guardroom flanked the gate.

The fort was completed in 1815 but it is uncertain if all the guns were mounted because seven years later, in 1822, Inch Fort was described as "a Sea battery with traverse circles for six traversing platforms; has four guns 24 pounders mounted on platforms".[14] On completion the fort could accommodate two officers, five NCOs and 80 soldiers but it never had a garrison of this size. Indeed in 1823, after eight years of peace, the garrison comprised a total of eight men: two gunners and six soldiers from a line battalion.[15]

4 Lough Foyle and Belfast Lough 1810–1816

The proposals for the fortification of Lough Foyle put forward by Sir George Hill and Thomas Knox in 1796 had come to nothing and no move was made to provide defences for Londonderry until the arrival of the Committee of Engineers in the early months of 1806. Brigadier General Mann RE, the senior member of the committee, put forward a plan to build two forts to defend the lough, each comprising a tower for two guns and a battery for five guns. One fort was to be sited at Greencastle on the Donegal shore and the other opposite it on Magilligan Point in County Londonderry.

The proposals languished in the files of the Board of Ordnance, partly because of the dilatoriness of the Board in dealing with them and partly because of delay in finalising the plans for the forts. In April 1810 Colonel Fisher RE wrote to the Inspector General of Fortifications concerning the design of the tower at Greencastle. "I have ventured to make an alteration in the Circular Tower proposed by the Committee, leaving out the projections and substituting a more simple profile."[1] It is not clear what the "projections" were, probably one or two machicolations, but the final design adopted was for an oval rather than a circular tower.

There were also problems concerning the construction of the tower and battery at Magilligan Point because of the loose shifting sand. Indeed Magilligan Point is, perhaps, unique in the British Isles in the way that the sand dunes advance and retreat considerable distances over quite short periods of time as a result of tidal action. It was probably the realisation of the high costs that would be incurred in providing adequate foundations for both the tower and the battery that resulted in the cancellation of the plan to build a fort at Magilligan. So only the tower for two guns was eventually built on a foundation provided by a grillage of timber.[2]

The Lough Foyle works were authorised on 5 November 1811 but it would seem that once again Colonel Fisher and Captain Sir William Smith had difficulty in obtaining the requisite competitive tenders necessary to satisfy the Respective Officers in Dublin. Certainly Mr Edgar of Londonderry was considered the only competent local contractor when he was awarded the contracts for the Lough Swilly forts. Determined to obtain proper competitive tenders, the Respective Officers appear to have looked further afield for contractors who might be interested in tendering for the Lough Foyle contracts. They must have advertised in the Dublin newspapers for it was a Dublin contractor, Mr Edward Farrell, who submitted the lowest tender and obtained the contracts in 1812. As is so often the case, it would have been better had the Board of Ordnance rejected the lowest tender since Farrell was unable to complete the contract according to the terms of his tender. By March 1813 he was insolvent, his workers unpaid and his creditors, including a number of prominent citizens of Londonderry, also unpaid.

On 27 March 1813 Captain Cardew RE, the officer supervising the works at Lough Swilly and Lough Foyle, was writing from Buncrana to Major General Fyers RE, the commanding engineer in Ireland, submitting a memorial from Farrell and another from his creditors. The memorial from Farrell's creditors requested the Respective Officers in Dublin to investigate the reason for the failure of the contractor to meet the terms of his contract and asking that, as it was quite clearly impossible to complete the contract at the prices he quoted in his tender, the Board of Ordnance should make good their losses, thus enabling the construction of the fort and the tower to be completed.

The problem stemmed from the fact that Edward Farrell had been completely misled as to the cost of materials in Londonderry and the cost of their transportation to the sites. Whether he was deliberately mis-advised or his informant was incompetent it is now impossible to judge. Suffice to say Farrell tendered basing his calculation on costs of timber at Greencastle at £10 per ton when the actual cost was £12 10s and in his own words he "sustained very heavy losses on almost every article of his contract too numerous in detail for your perusal".[3] He had already expended £4,000 more on the works at Greencastle than he had received and most of this sum was owed to nine "respectable opulent merchants".[4]

In Captain Cardew's opinion the best answer was to adjust the contract and bring it into line with the Lough Swilly contracts. He pointed out that as it was, Farrell would not be able to finish the works and there was virtually no likelihood that any other contractor would take the contract over on the original terms. In addition, he felt that the Board of Ordnance had a moral responsibility since the workers had continued working and the merchants advancing credit under the belief that as it was a government contract it would not fail.[5] The Ordnance papers do not reveal what the eventual outcome of the memorials was but the fort at Greencastle and the tower at Magilligan were finally completed in 1816–17.

The fort at Greencastle was designed as a tower for two guns and a battery for five 24-pdr SB guns sited 35 feet (10.76 metres) above the level of the lough, while the tower and living quarters were a further 50 feet (15.38 metres) above the battery. Two guns were mounted on the distinctive oval-shaped tower, and when the fort was completed these guns were two 24-pdr SB carronades on traversing platforms and using individual pivots.

The tower was built of regular ashlar on a base of squared rubble masonry, the improved standard of workmanship of the upper works of the tower perhaps reflecting a change for the better in Edward Farrell's fortunes. The tower stood 35 feet (10.76 metres) high and was not shaped as a true oval but was more of a squashed cam shape. It was also unusual in that the northern and southern ends of the parapet sloped down in a half circle at an angle of approximately 45 degrees for a distance of about seven feet (2.15 metres), a feature found in no other Martello tower and which may have been designed to cause enemy round shot to ricochet off the tower rather than strike square on to the parapet

On the north-east side overlooking the entrance to the fort and on the south-east side facing towards the lough there were two large windows and each was flanked by two apertures for ventilation. There was a stone staircase

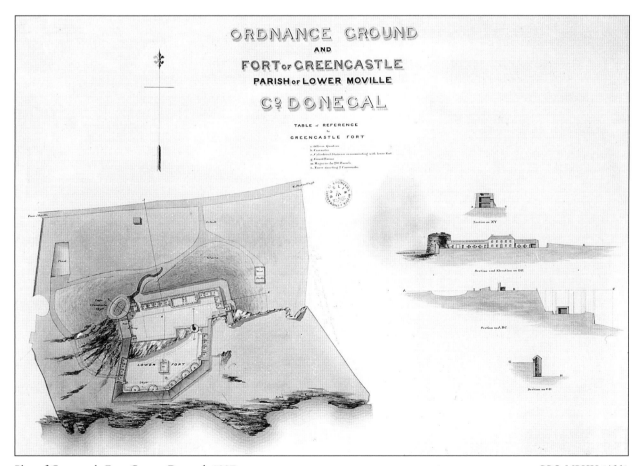

Plan of Greencastle Fort, County Donegal. 1827.

PRO MPHH 1/641

Greencastle Fort showing the tower which mounted two 24-pdr carronades.   *Author's collection*

Greencastle Fort from Magilligan Point.   *Author*

linking the first floor with the gun platform while the basement was entered through two trapdoors and down ladders. In the basement was the magazine but there was also a firing gallery for riflemen using four loopholes almost level with the bottom of the tower. These loopholes and the window above defended the approach to the main gate which was situated adjacent to the tower.

Inside the fort, abutting on the middle of the rear wall, there was a two-storey building which provided accommodation and mess facilities for the officers of the garrison and on either side of this building along the northern side wall of the upper fort there was single-storey barrack accommodation for the soldiers. Above the level of the roof of the soldier's accommodation the rear wall was loopholed for musketry and the roof itself acted as a banquette and walkway for the troops manning the loopholes.

The entrance to the fort was by means of a sunken road through a glacis leading to an arched gateway. Between the gateway and the wall of the tower were two more loopholes angled to enable musketry fire to be brought down upon any enemy at the base of the tower. A ditch ran parallel with the rear wall of the fort and for a short distance at the north end. The upper and lower portions of the fort were linked by a staircase enclosed in a stone tower, the circular top of which stood on the upper level opposite the officer's accommodation.

The main battery had positions for five guns on traversing platforms firing through embrasures. Behind the battery terreplein there was a large stone magazine which could hold four hundred barrels of gunpowder. The side walls of the main battery were lined with casemates forming arcades on each side and above each arcade was a loopholed wall with a banquette. Surprisingly, there

Magilligan Martello Tower.   *Author*

was no shot furnace at the rear of the terreplein but it is possible one or two portable grates were provided.

The fort was very similar in area to Knockalla Fort but was less heavily armed, mounting four guns fewer and these were 24-pdr SB guns rather than 42-pdr SB guns at Knockalla. However, the design of Greencastle Fort was obviously considered to be particularly successful and Colonel George Lewis RE used an almost identical design as an illustration for 'A Fort at the Entrance of a Harbour' in an article in 1844 for the *Professional Papers of the Royal Engineers*.[6]

Across the lough, immediately opposite Greencastle, work continued on Magilligan Point building the Martello tower. The original plan had been to build a tower and battery at Magilligan similar to that at Greencastle. However, Major General Mann RE decided that a single tower would be adequate to cooperate with Greencastle Fort. In 1810 he wrote: "The work on Magilligan Point is meant to co-operate by producing a

The gun platform of Magilligan Martello Tower showing the entrance to the stairs (left) and the two entrances to the shot furnace (centre and right).   *Author*

Drop Fire and also to scour its own shore and for these purposes the Tower only may be sufficient."[7]

Without a ditch, the tower stood about 200 yards (185 metres) from the water's edge. It was a standard Irish-pattern circular tower for two 'long' 24-pdr SB guns mounted on traversing platforms using a single rear-mounted pivot. This design of tower was peculiar to Ireland because in the rest of Britain, Martello towers were built either to an elliptical design mounting one 24-pdr 'long' gun or to the cam-shaped design for an armament of one 'long' 24-pdr and two 24-pdr carronades or two 5.5-inch (140-mm) SB howitzers. In Ireland, towers generally similar to that at Magilligan Point were to be found at Macamish Point in Lough Swilly, on Ireland's Eye Island to the north of Dublin, and at Sandymount, south of Dublin.

The tower was built between 1812 and 1817 and is best described by quoting the Ordnance Survey Memoir for the parish of Magilligan, written in July 1835:

It is of circular form, 166 feet 10 inches [51.33 metres] in circumference measured above the basement, which is sunk 16 feet [4.9 metres] deep. The walls are 11 feet [3.3 metres] thick above and 13 feet [4 metres] below the basement of cut freestone from the quarries in Ballyharrigan in the parish of Bovevagh. It mounts one gun, which turns on a pivot and can be presented to any quarter. In the centre of the tower there is an excellent spring.[8]

The tower was 36 feet (11.07 metres) high and was originally designed to mount two guns, though by 1835 it would seem it only mounted one. The tower had no central pillar but had supporting cross-walls on each floor. The magazine was designed to hold two hundred

barrels of gunpowder and the original copper door with bronze hinges can be seen in the tower today. Recessed into the parapet there was a shot furnace with two entrances and other recesses for made-up ammunition. As with all Martello towers, the entrance was at first-floor level and was reached by means of a ladder. Above the entrance there was a machicolation which enabled the garrison to fire down on an enemy attacking the door. There was a window on each side of the tower but the side facing the lough was unbroken and, therefore, the strongest. Inside the tower, communication between all levels was by means of a staircase built within the rear wall.

Because of the problems with the contractor, and no doubt because the war against Napoleon was moving towards victory for the Allies, work on the fort and the tower was prolonged. During this time, either because the country remained unsettled or simply to provide security against theft of materials, troops were required to protect "the works of defence carrying [sic] on by the Ordnance Department, which the country people would otherwise interrupt and destroy".[9] So huts were constructed for an officer and 20 soldiers at Greencastle and Magilligan. By 1816 the works were almost complete and although Greencastle Fort had accommodation for three officers, eight NCOs and 160 soldiers, its garrison in that year was actually a Master Gunner, one Royal Artillery NCO and six gunners together with two officers, six NCOs and 90 soldiers of the line. Seven years later that number had been reduced to a total of three gunners.

Further down the coast, Belfast remained something of a backwater as far as defences were concerned despite its increasing importance as a manufacturing centre and commercial port. By the end of the Napoleonic War in 1815 very little had been done in the way of improving the defences of Belfast Lough, other than maintaining Carrickfergus Castle. Although the castle remained the main, indeed only, defence for Belfast Lough, it was poorly situated and armed for the role. The main armament of the castle, the 12-pdr SB guns, lacked the range to reach the navigable channel in the lough. At Carrickfergus the lough was 6,160 yards (5,686 metres) wide and the channel was more than 3,000 yards (2,760 metres) distant from the castle. The maximum range of the 12-pdr gun was only 1,800 yards (1,650 metres) and at that distance it was unlikely that the shot would make a significant impact on a warship of any real size.

Despite the inadequacies of the armament, some steps were taken to strengthen Carrickfergus Castle in the early

Carrickfergus Castle, looking towards the Grand Battery from the north.   *Author*

years of the nineteenth century by increasing the number of guns and making some of the accommodation and stores bomb-proof together with other alterations. These included filling up the ground floor of each of the half-moon towers flanking the main gate with rubble and earth and providing a machicolation over the gateway between the two towers.

By 1811 the number of guns had been increased with the addition of six 12-pdr SB guns bringing the total number of that calibre of gun to 20. The castle retained the two 6-pdr and six 4-pdr guns, giving a grand total of 28 guns. The bulk of these guns were mounted, firing through 14 embrasures along the eastern wall of the castle. Seven were mounted on the Grand Battery adjoining the main gate, with a further seven mounted at intervals along the rest of the wall. All the guns were on garrison carriages and not traversing platforms, which perhaps indicates that the Board of Ordnance was quite well aware of the castle's limitations as a coastal defence fortress. In 1811 a report on the condition of the guns and carriages stated: "one carriage No 5 on the Grand Battery is very much out of repair and three others unserviceable. The two 6 pounder and three 4 pounder carriages also unserviceable. All guns and carriages in need of painting".[10]

During this time the Grand Battery was reinforced by the construction of bomb-proof vaults underneath which acted as stores but could also be used as protected accommodation for the garrison. In 1811 a small expense magazine was completed at the southern end of the Inner Ward of the castle, probably to cater for the increase in the number of guns.

The castle remained a major barracks for troops with accommodation for four officers, ten NCOs and 200 soldiers. In July 1813 authority was received to build "two barrack rooms for the Artillery . . . which accommodation is become necessary in consequence of the Troops having quitted the Great Tower of the castle". The cost of the two barrack rooms came to £200 18s 5¾d.[11] The troops were removed from the tower in order to provide additional storerooms for artillery and ordnance stores. In 1815 the tower was provided with an arched roof and the ground floor converted into a vaulted magazine for 935 barrels of gunpowder. In 1816 the tower was used to store the arms of the disbanded militia and volunteers of the district and the ammunition of the troops in the north of Ireland. At one time 10,000 stands of arms were stored in the tower.

5 The Irish Signal Towers

The renewal of war with France in 1803 and the continued state of unrest in Ireland led, as we have seen in the earlier chapters, to the fortification of parts of the coast against invasion. Since the strength of the Army in Ireland was insufficient to protect all those parts of the coast vulnerable to an enemy landing, it followed that early information of the arrival of an invasion force would be vital. This information could only be provided if there was an effective and fast method of communication linking Army headquarters in Dublin with the threatened parts of the coast.

Because of the extremely poor and sometimes quite appalling roads in Ireland, a courier could take days to reach Dublin from the south and west coasts, the areas most threatened with invasion, so another answer to the problem had to be found. In France, in the early 1790s, Claud Chappé had developed a visual telegraph system using a semaphore which, by the end of the century, connected Paris with a number of major cities, including Lille, Brest and Toulon, and enabled messages to be transmitted very quickly. The British soon followed the French example and by 1796 a telegraph system using six shutters on a large frame was set up to enable the Admiralty in London to communicate with the naval bases at Portsmouth and Chatham and with the Kent coast. This system had been extended as far as Plymouth by 1806.

A more primitive signalling system using a flag and a number of black balls on a mast was set up at the same time along the south and east coasts between Land's End and Yarmouth. This system was designed to enable the signal stations to communicate with warships at sea rather than with each other and, when compared with Murray's six-shutter telegraph system, was very limited in the number and variety of messages that could be transmitted. Communication was only possible by day and then only when the visibility was good. By night there was provision for a beacon to be lit but, clearly, the beacon could only be used to signal a major emergency such as an actual landing by the French.

In October 1803 Richard Lovell Edgeworth, an Irish landowner and father of Maria Edgeworth the novelist, submitted a plan for a telegraph system using triangular pointers, to link Dublin with major points on the coast. He was asked to set up a system to link Dublin, Athlone and Galway and this system was ready by June 1804. The intermediate signal stations were manned by the Edgeworthstown Yeomanry who were converted to a Yeomanry Telegraphic Corps and messages were said to have taken only eight minutes to be transmitted between Dublin and Galway.

A short time before Richard Edgeworth submitted his proposal for a telegraph system it had become clear to Lord Hardwick, the lord lieutenant, that Ireland needed a chain of coastal signal stations similar to that on the English coast. By 7 June 1803 he was writing to Lord Hawksbury, Secretary of State for the Home Department, in London giving his opinion that:

> the advantages arising from the establishment of a regular service of Signal Stations on the Coast of Ireland similar to those which were erected on the Eastern coast of England in the year 1798 were so clear after the renewal of the war I felt it my duty to bring the subject under consideration of His Majesty's Ministers . . . with a view to the adoption of some plan, for the execution of such works, under the authority of the Board of Admiralty and the Board of Ordnance.[1]

In 1803 Rear Admiral Whitshed RN had been appointed naval adviser to the lord lieutenant with specific responsibility for all matters directly relating to the defence of the coast. It would appear that in addition to setting up 20 Sea Fencible districts he was also responsible for the execution of the plan to establish the chain of signal stations which eventually stretched along most of the Irish coast, sited on virtually every headland from Dublin round the south and west coasts to Malin Head in the north. Only the stretches of coast between Londonderry and Belfast and that along the east coast from Belfast to Dublin were not included in the chain, nor provided with other defences.

The actual proposal for signal stations in Ireland seems to date from August 1803 when plans were authorised for

Malin Head signal tower, 1812: a sketch by Captain Sir William Smith. *The Board of Trinity College Dublin*

Carrigan Head signal tower, County Donegal. The tower stands on the precipitous Slieve League cliffs near Killybegs. *Author*

the construction of signal stations and flag staffs in west Cork, probably linked to the establishment of a naval base in Bantry Bay for Rear Admiral Sir Robert Calder's squadron. In a letter to London, Lord Hardwick explained that each of the signal stations in Ireland would require a defensible stone building. Indeed, on 21 September 1803 Lieutenant Colonel Beckwith (secretary to the Commander-in-Chief in Ireland) wrote to Colonel Fisher RE explaining in detail what the Commander-in-Chief required: "I am therefore to suggest the expediency of constructing at the stations where the signal posts may be found necessary, buildings of stone capable of lodging six men, with a distinct apartment for the officer, and defensible by that number."[2] Indeed, Beckwith went on to suggest the construction of round towers about 20 feet (6.16 metres) high, mounting two or three blunderbusses or swivel stocks.[3] Since the object was stated as being "merely defence against the attempts of the disaffected", it was felt that there was no need to go to the expense of constructing Martello towers, though two were subsequently built in Wexford as combined gun towers and signal stations.[4]

Each signal station was to be manned by a Royal Navy lieutenant, usually one that was on half-pay, a midshipman and a signal party of two or three sailors. These latter were frequently found from the local Sea Fencible district. In addition there was a small guard provided by the local Yeomanry or Fencible infantry regiment or, occasionally, from a nearby regular infantry battalion. The unsettled nature of conditions in Ireland necessitated the provision of a protection party and the signal station building was designed, in the words of

Lieutenant Colonel Beckwith, "to prevent the destruction of the signal posts without the necessity of protecting them by strong detachments".[5]

Although the Commander-in-Chief's original suggestion was for round towers, the vast majority of signal stations in Ireland were eventually two-storey square towers. Edmund Wakefield, in *An Account of Ireland, Statistical and Political*, published in 1812, describes one signal station – that at Kerry Head in County Kerry – as follows:

> The Signal Station consists of a square tower thirty four feet [10.46 metres] in height, each side of which is thirteen feet [4 metres] wide. It is committed to the care of a lieutenant and a guard. The door is in the upper storey, the only access to it by means of a small ladder, which can be handed up in a moment. It is built of stone and might be defended by half a dozen men against any number unless provided with cannon.[6]

The towers, with a few exceptions, all had a flat roof surrounded by a parapet from which projected three machicolations. The whole structure was surrounded by a rectangular enclosure with a fan-shaped extension on the seaward side, in the centre of which was the socket for the signal mast. The enclosure was formed by a stone wall and provided a form of defensive perimeter for the signal station. However, in a number of locations which were particularly difficult to access, such as Carrigan Head in Donegal, there was no enclosure.

A total of 81 towers was built and these were numbered from No 1 at Pigeon House in Dublin to No 81 at Malin Head in Donegal. In Ulster, signal stations were only built in County Donegal, 12 in total. These were: No 70, St John's Head; No 71, Carrigan Head; No 72, Malin

Malin Head signal tower
and the remains of the
World War Two
coastwatchers post as they
are today.

Author

Beg; No 73, Glen Head; No 74, Dawros Head; No 75, Crohy Head; No 76, Mullaghderg Hill; No 77, Bloody Foreland; No 78, Horn Head; No 79, Melmore Head; No 80, Fanad Head; and No 81, Malin Head.

Work started on the towers in 1804 and all were completed by 1806 and by that year signal lieutenants had been appointed to all but Nos 74, 76, 77 and 78.[7] The cost of building the Donegal towers averaged approximately £600 each, the most expensive being the almost inaccessible tower at Carrigan Head where the cost was £690. Captain Sir William Smith, the assistant engineer, visited the signal stations at Malin Head and Fanad Head in 1804 and his sketches show that at each there was only a signal mast and a wooden hut to accommodate the signallers. However, his later sketches of Malin Head in 1808 and Fanad Head in 1812 show the completed signal tower at each location.

The limited capability of the coastal towers to communicate with each other meant that there was little enthusiasm for maintaining them once the immediate threat of invasion was over. In 1809 Admiral Whitshed was instructed to abandon 48 of the stations, leaving only Nos 23 to 51, between Cork and Inisheer Island in Galway Bay, and the Melmore, Fanad and Malin Head towers at the entrance to Lough Swilly remaining in operation. Although some of the abandoned stations were

reactivated during the war with the United States from 1812 to 1815, all were finally abandoned by 1816 and allowed to fall into ruin, although at least one has recently been converted into a private house.

The towers were never used again but in World War Two, or 'The Emergency' as it was called in neutral Éire, a coast-watching service was set up around the Irish coast to warn of enemy ships and aircraft. Eighty-eight concrete observation posts were constructed, many alongside the old Napoleonic towers, and in 1943 all coast-watching posts were ordered to cut a large-lettered sign 'EIRE' and the number of the post on the ground as near as practicable to the post. These markings were made at the request of the United States Army Air Force as a navigational aid to help prevent infringements of Irish Free State airspace.

Each coast-watching team comprised a corporal and seven or eight men who worked an eight-hour or twelve-hour shift in pairs, reporting all shipping and aircraft movements in their areas of observation together with other events such as drifting mines or dead bodies. The Coast-Watching Service was disbanded at the end of the war and today many of these concrete observation posts can still be seen, including, in Donegal, the ones at Carrigan Head and Malin Head.

The Years of Peace 6 1816–1854

As happens after every great conflict when the fighting ends, the nation heaves a collective sigh of relief and quickly reduces all military expenditure. Disregarding the Chinese military sage Sun Tze's adage that a state may not need an army for a thousand years but dare not be without it for a single day, the British government moved quickly to reduce the size of both the Royal Navy and the Army. The government also ensured that the Board of Ordnance reduced expenditure on fortifications and barracks and, in turn, the number of troops allocated to man the forts and batteries was quickly reduced to the minimum required to maintain the armament.

Ireland, however, remained an uneasy country and the Board felt that the fortifications there could not be left unmanned since it was probable that 'the peasantry' would strip them of everything that could be removed if there was no guard on the Board's property. Londonderry and Belfast remained the two main garrison stations in Ulster though the artillerymen for the forts and batteries were provided from the artillery units stationed at Islandbridge, near Dublin. Islandbridge was the Royal Artillery headquarters in Ireland at that time and from there companies of artillery were detached to man the major coastal fortifications in Ireland at Cork, Bantry Bay, Duncannon, along the Shannon and in Ulster.

In 1823 the garrisons of the forts along the shores of Lough Swilly and Lough Foyle were reduced to a bare minimum with only two or three Royal Artillery gunners and a few infantry soldiers allocated to each. In a report dated May 1823, for example, the garrison of Dunree Fort comprised one NCO and two gunners of the Royal Artillery and eight infantrymen, while at Knockalla Fort there were two gunners and nine infantrymen. Greencastle Fort was the only fort without a detachment from a line battalion , having just three gunners as its garrison.[1]

Ten years later, in 1833, these garrisons were reduced still further as all the detachments from infantry battalions had been withdrawn. The fort at Rathmullen was in the hands of a storekeeper and seven gunners while at Macamish there were seven gunners with a further seven under the command of a Master Gunner at Dunree. All these gunners were drawn from a Royal Artillery company under the command of a captain which was stationed at Buncrana.

It is, perhaps, appropriate to include here a brief description of the role of the Master Gunner. This office was a very old one and from the time of the invention of guns there were Master Gunners in charge of them. In general, the duties of a Master Gunner included the supervision of the ordnance, carriages, ammunition and stores in his charge, ensuring that they were preserved in good order; he was required to report any defects he could not repair himself. According to a contemporary document, his subsidiary duties included keeping the battery clean, firing salutes if ordered to do so and raising the flag. In addition he was required to render accounts and returns of the ordnance and stores in his charge to the Principal Storekeeper's Office at the Tower of London.[2] The role of the Master Gunner became much reduced with the advent of artillery officers but in coastal fortresses he remained until the very end a specialist artilleryman responsible for the care and maintenance of the guns and stores.

By 1839 the Lough Swilly and Lough Foyle forts were no longer occupied by troops, and by 1844 the sole occupants of Dunree, Knockalla and Carrickfergus Castle were the Master Gunners. There is no indication that they had any subordinates to assist them for by that date the artillery company at Buncrana had been withdrawn. However, some years earlier, in 1835, the Master Gunner at Carrickfergus Castle was assisted by two Invalid gunners from the Invalid Detachment, Royal Artillery at Woolwich. This unit was the successor to the Invalid Battalion, Royal Artillery and comprised a number of artillery pensioners who were still able to carry out duties of a static nature. In 1851 a single Invalid gunner was stationed at Inch Fort, a marked improvement on the situation pertaining up to that point with the forts and batteries at Ned's Point, Rathmullen, Macamish and Inch having been the responsibility of a Bombardier Jackson RA who resided in the married quarter at Ned's Point.

So reduced was the number of gunners and engineers in

1850 that the Ordnance papers of that year speak of Master Gunner Armstrong at Knockalla Fort, who was also responsible for Rathmullen and Macamish, travelling on engineer duties as authorised by the senior engineer officer at Londonderry. Also in 1850 the Ordnance papers show that the Master Gunner at Greencastle Fort petitioned the Inspector General of Fortifications in London for permission to sow grass on a piece of Ordnance land he rented. This indicates the level of minor detail with which the Inspector General found himself dealing at this time. Perhaps the most enterprising of the Master Gunners was the one at Carrickfergus Castle who, in 1840, supplemented his rather meagre pay, albeit illegally, by permitting the public to enter the Great Tower of the castle on receipt of admission money. He was required to make good the cost of the visitors depredations.[3]

In the period of almost 40 years between 1816 and 1854 very little was done to maintain the forts and batteries in Ulster. The Ordnance papers contain reports that repairs were needed, particularly to the roofs of the towers, and complaints of dampness were frequent. Indeed, in 1848 the grand sum of £50 6s 7¾d was expended to improve the drainage on top of all the Lough Swilly towers.[4]

It was obvious that money was very tight throughout this period, for year after year the same defects were recorded in the engineer's inspection reports. At Macamish battery, for example, in 1842 "the iron racer for one of the Traversing Platforms at this fort that was reported last year as 'not correctly laid down' is not yet altered" and repairs reported in 1841 as being needed at Rathmullen were also not yet completed in 1842.[5]

It seems that this failure to carry out repairs reflected not only the government's lack of interest in maintaining fortifications generally, but also resulted from the fact that the building of new barracks and the improvement of old ones was the Board of Ordnance's main priority at this time. Indeed, in 1842 the only major engineer project being undertaken in the whole of the Ulster District was the construction of Ebrington Barracks in Londonderry.

The armament of all the forts remained unaltered until the 1840s when proposals for a number of changes were put forward. In 1845 it was suggested that the efficacy of Dunree and Greencastle forts would be improved if the existing armament of 24-pdr SB guns was replaced by the heavier 56-pdr SB guns. In addition it was proposed that the two 24-pdr SB guns on the tower at Dunree Fort should be replaced by two 5.5-inch (140-mm) iron howitzers. Two years later this proposal had still not been acted upon and in that year the decision was taken simply to replace the old

guns in the main armament of Dunree with new guns of the same type. However, the two 24-pdr SB guns were removed from the tower and two howitzers mounted in their place. No action was taken to replace any of the guns at Greencastle Fort but at Knockalla the common traversing platforms for the 42-pdr SB guns were replaced by dwarf traversing platforms.[6] One other small alteration was carried out, this time at Inch Fort in order to improve the mounting of the guns on the tower. Here the banquette on the tower was raised a few inches to reduce the incline of the traversing platforms which had been too high.[7]

In 1845 the armament of Carrickfergus Castle still consisted of the old 12-pdr SB guns, though the need to replace them had been recognised for a number of years. In 1853 the matter appeared to have been shelved despite the fact that 12 of the 13 guns then mounted were considered to be unserviceable. The Inspector General of Fortifications was fully aware of the inadequacy of the existing armament, however, since he minuted:

> The Castle of Carrickfergus forms a very inadequate defence for Belfast Lough, but as an existing work and commanding a certain amount of anchorage it is certainly desirable to go to the extent of giving it a better armament than the very imperfect one it at present possesses.[8]

At Enniskillen, Belleek and Ballyshannon little was done in this period other than to maintain the barracks. However, at Enniskillen two buildings were erected within the western redoubt for use as a military hospital but the redoubt kept its armament of four iron howitzers and was retained as an outwork to defend the bridge and the approach to Castle Barracks from the west.

The long period of peace came to a close with the start of the Crimean War. Although the war had little immediate effect as far as the fortifications in Ulster were concerned, it did see the formation of three militia artillery units. The problem of providing gunners to man all the fortifications in the United Kingdom was almost insuperable, certainly in peacetime, though this was a problem successive governments preferred to ignore until shortly before the outbreak of the war. The modern militia had been raised by act of parliament in 1852 and included a Corps of Militia Artillery. Three units were formed in Ulster: the Antrim Artillery Militia, the Donegal Artillery Militia, and the Londonderry Artillery Militia.

The Antrim Artillery Militia was based at Carrickfergus Castle and trained with and manned the guns of the castle. The Donegal Artillery Militia had its headquarters at

Lifford but did send detachments to train at Dunree Fort and Buncrana. The third unit, the Londonderry Artillery Militia, was a field artillery unit at this time and does not appear to have been involved in manning the defences of Lough Foyle. All three artillery units were embodied for periods during the Crimean War between 1854 and 1856.

The outbreak of war with Russia in 1854 brought to an end a period of peace that had lasted 39 years. It also ushered in a new era filled with a host of new uncertainties, for the war heralded a period of huge technological advances in military equipment. These included the advent of armoured plate and rifled and breech-loading guns for both ships and forts, together with steam propulsion for ships. These and other scientific advances were to usher in a period of constant change as regards coastal fortification which was to last until the end of the century.

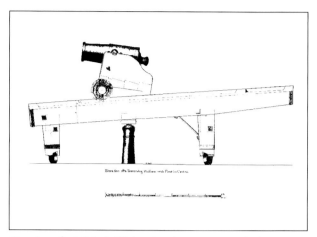

Drawing of a 5.5-inch SB iron howitzer on a central pivot common traversing platform. *Author's collection*

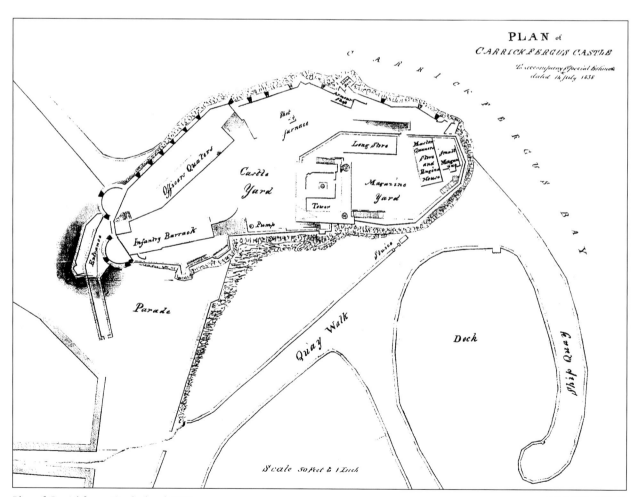

Plan of Carrickfergus Castle dated 1838. *PRO WO 55/842*

Fear of France and the Technological Revolution 1855–1880

The military fiasco of the Crimean War brought about the demise of the Board of Ordnance in 1855. The Board had had a long and honourable history but financial independence and its overly bureaucratic method of operation, together with its mismanagement of the provision of equipment during the war, had raised a barrage of public criticism. The sufferings of the troops at the siege of Sevastopol provoked an outcry at home which resulted in a parliamentary committee to inquire into the general administration of the Army. The Board had not been unaware of the rapid technological advances then being made in both guns and armour but its organisation was such that it found it almost impossible to meet the urgent requirements of actual war. Amongst the parliamentary committee's recommendations was the abolition of the Board of Ordnance and, weakened politically, the Master General of the Ordnance and the Board were unable to resist. The Board was abolished and,

as a result, the Royal Regiment of Artillery and the Corps of Royal Engineers were transferred to the control of the War Office under the combined command of the Secretary of State for War and the Commander-in-Chief.

The Crimean War had demonstrated to the British public not only the fact that the administration of the armed forces of the Crown was in need of radical overhaul but also the inescapable fact that France under Napoleon III had become, once again, a major force in European politics. French troops had distinguished themselves at the siege of Sevastopol, French armoured floating batteries had been used against the Russians at Kinburn and the French navy was deeply interested in the use of steam propulsion and was adopting the shell guns designed by General Paixhans. A huge new naval base was being constructed at Cherbourg and, in addition, three years after the end of the Crimean War, the French army defeated the Austrians in a number of bloody battles in northern Italy.

The ships

By the time the Crimean War ended, steam propulsion had been in use in the Royal Navy for over 20 years. Initially it was primarily used to power small paddle tugs which manoeuvred the sailing warships in harbour when the wind was foul. The Royal Navy believed that the large paddle wheels, which were the normal method of propelling steamships at this time, would be very vulnerable to enemy fire and by the end of the 1840s those warships powered by steam were mainly paddle sloops and small paddle frigates. The 1850s saw the advent of screw propulsion and its adoption by both the Royal Navy and the French navy as an auxiliary means of propulsion for larger warships. By 1858 the Royal Navy had 29 screw line of battle ships, a total equalled by the French navy, but all were still wooden hulled.

However, the apparent invulnerability of their iron-plated floating batteries which had been so successful in the Crimean War had not been lost on the French. In 1859

the French navy laid down the first ironclad major warship, *La Gloire*, which was to be followed by three more sister-ships. Although only clad with iron on top of a wooden hull, the armour was impenetrable to solid shot and at a stroke the French navy had overtaken the Royal Navy. Alarmist pamphlets were published and circulated in England including one in which a French naval officer was quoted as saying: "She [France] has command of the Channel at the present moment."[1]

The British answer to the French threat followed swiftly. In 1860 HMS *Warrior*, the first warship to be built entirely of iron with additional armour was launched. This ship and her sister-ship HMS *Black Prince* had an armoured belt of iron 4.5 inches (112 mm) thick backed by a further 18 inches (457 mm) of teak. When completed, the two ships were the most powerful and also the largest warships in any navy. Both ships were steam-propelled and a speed of 14 knots was achieved.

HMS *Warrior*: the refurbished battleship is preserved as a museum ship at Portsmouth.

Author

These ships revolutionised naval tactics since they were fast, no longer reliant upon uncertain winds, and heavily armed. However, they lacked endurance when using steam power alone and so coaling stations had to be established around the world and these had to be protected and secured from enemy attack.

The American Civil War between 1861 and 1865 saw the development of ironclad warships termed monitors by the United States Navy, and these vessels provided practical evidence of the effectiveness of naval armour against solid shot and shells fired by smooth-bore guns. The monitors had an armoured belt comprising two 1-inch (25-mm) thick layers of iron plate backed by 8 inches (200 mm) of wooden planking on the hull. The armour of the two turrets was even thicker and consisted of eight layers of 1-inch (25-mm) iron plate bolted together with overlapping joints and lined with an additional layer of iron. The total thickness came to 9 inches (225 mm) of iron plate.

Suddenly ships had become invulnerable to the fire of standard coast defence artillery and the introduction of turrets enabled the largest calibre of guns to be mounted and fired almost independently of the direction of the ship. In the 11 years from 1859 to 1870 the forerunners of the modern battleship entered service.

The guns

There had been little change in the design of guns over the previous 150 years and in the early nineteenth century the standard gun with which the coastal forts were armed was the 'long' 24-pdr SB gun of 50 cwt. By the 1830s the preferred weapon was the heavier 32-pdr SB of 56 cwt even though there was little difference in the effective range of the two guns. Both relied upon the effect of a solid projectile, or shot, sometimes heated to red-heat, striking a wooden-hulled warship. Although a rudimentary form of explosive shell existed at this time, it was only used in howitzers and mortars, both of which fired at a high angle. Because of the long time of flight of the shell it was difficult for these weapons to hit a moving target.

In 1821 General Paixhans of the French army developed a gun intended to fire shells. The Paixhans gun was tested successfully against a ship at Brest in 1821 and again in 1824 but it took a further 13 years before shell guns were adopted by the French. Spurred on by the French example, and fearful again of being left behind technologically, the British developed smooth-bore shell guns of their own and by 1839 had produced three guns "a la Paixhans", as Colonel Lewis RE described them in 1841. These were the 56-pdr, 68-pdr and 84-pdr guns, the latter two also being known as the 8-inch (203-mm) and 10-inch (254-mm) shell guns. The 10-inch (254-mm) shell gun was considered to be primarily a naval weapon and only a few were used in coastal forts.[2]

The 56-pdr was 11 feet (3.38 metres) long and weighed 97 cwt and so was considered only suitable "to the Salients of Coast Batteries and to Cavaliers or heights of the Sea Defences of Fortresses, to be always mounted *en barbette* on ground platforms or low traversing platforms".[3] Like the 10-inch (254-mm) shell gun, this weapon was not used in any great numbers. The preferred shell gun was the 8-inch (203-mm) of 50 cwt and 6 feet 8.5 inches (2.06 metres) long. This gun was 560 lbs (254.5 kg) lighter than the 32-pdr SB gun and like the latter could be mounted on a standard pattern traversing platform.

The last and largest smooth-bore gun to enter service with the British Army was the 68-pdr, a cast-iron gun of 95 cwt which entered service in 1841 and which by 1855 was a principal part of the main armament of all major coast defence forts. Even as it entered service, however, experiments with guns with rifled barrels were taking place. Rifled guns seemed to be the answer to providing guns with the greater muzzle-velocity required in order for solid shot and shells to penetrate the new armour now coming into service. While the effect of an exploding shell on a wooden warship was normally devastating, such a missile had very little effect when used against the new ironclads and fired from a smooth-bore gun. To obtain the higher velocity needed for a shell to penetrate, not only was a rifled barrel necessary but also a much stronger chamber to withstand increased charges.

A number of artillery experts, including Emperor Napoleon III, had been attempting to develop an effective rifled gun. A number of British 68-pdr cast-iron guns were rifled according to a principle devised by Mr CW Lancaster and were used at the siege of Sevastopol in the Crimean War. The barrels of these guns were made oval and twisted in the bore and, not entirely surprisingly, proved unsuccessful as the projectiles often jammed in the bore. After the war, Napoleon III had a number of brass field pieces rifled and these were used with considerable success in Algeria. The system was simpler than Lancaster's, the rifling comprising six shallow grooves into which fitted two bands of studs around a cylindrical projectile. As a result the French army decided to rifle all field artillery according to this system.

The French interest in rifled ordnance was matched in England by the work of a number of inventors including Armstrong, Whitworth and Blakely. Guns had traditionally been manufactured of cast iron but this metal had serious limitations, being deficient in tensile strength, thus restricting the size of the gunpowder charge. Steel was not dependable at this date so the gun makers turned to using wrought iron. Armstrong developed a rifled breech-loading (RBL) gun as early as 1854 and this gun was notable for the fact that instead of being cast in one piece, as were the smooth-bore guns, it was built-up by means of shrinking a number of wrought-iron tubes, one upon another, to provide the necessary strength. After four years of trials an Ordnance committee recommended the adoption of this gun and in 1859 Armstrong was appointed Superintendent of the Royal Gun Factory at Woolwich.

There is some doubt as to whether this method was Armstrong's own idea or whether he pirated the design from Captain Alexander Blakely. Certainly Blakely patented a method of constructing gun barrels in layers only to have his design ridiculed by the Board of Ordnance. Armstrong, however, presented his patents, gratis, to the Crown on completion of the successful trials of his gun and was immediately granted a knighthood.

Rifled guns were also developed by Joseph Whitworth who produced breech-loading guns with his own hexagonal rifling. These guns were produced between 1854 and 1857 and their construction differed from that of Armstrong's gun in that they were constructed of wrought-iron cylindrical tubes forced over each other by hydraulic pressure rather than by heating and shrinking. The performance of these guns was impressive and in every way comparable with Armstrong's guns but despite this the War Office took the decision to adopt the latter, probably influenced by the fact that the Crown already held the patents.

Armstrong's breech-loading system was not a success and there were a number of accidents because of a weakness in sealing the breech. Added to this was the fact that in trials the Armstrong 7-inch (177-mm) RBL gun, designed for use both by the Royal Navy and in coastal fortresses, proved to be less effective against armour than the 68-pdr SB gun. It was for this reason that in 1864 a further trial was ordered by the War Office to compare the performance of breech-loaders and muzzle-loaders. Both Armstrong and Whitworth had taken the precaution of developing a muzzle-loading rifled gun and in the trial all the guns, including an Armstrong RBL with a modified breech action, performed satisfactorily. However, the committee reported in 1865 that the muzzle-loaders were superior to the breech-loaders in all respects, including ease of working the gun and cost of construction.

This series of trials over a period of ten years confirmed the superiority of rifled ordnance but both the Royal Navy and the Army held vast numbers of cast-iron smooth-bore guns including over 10,000 32-pdrs of various weights and 8-inch (203-mm) shell guns. Various attempts had been made to rifle smooth-bore guns without success but in 1862 Major Palliser RA suggested a practical system. Tubes of coiled wrought iron were fitted inside the cast-iron barrels of the smooth-bore guns and rifled. This system was used to produce two types of 64-pdr converted guns: the 64-pdr RML of 71 cwt which was converted from the 8-inch (203mm) shell gun; and the 64-pdr RML of 58 cwt. This latter gun was converted from the 3,000 32-pdr SB guns of 58 and 56 cwt. In addition, a number of 68-pdr SBML guns were converted to 80-pdr RML guns of 5 tons.

By 1870 rifled muzzle-loading guns had superceded Armstrong's rifled breech-loading guns but a number of

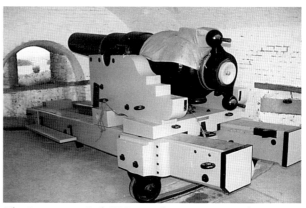

The Armstrong 7-inch RBL gun: this gun is mounted at Fort Nelson on the outskirts of Portsmouth.   *Author*

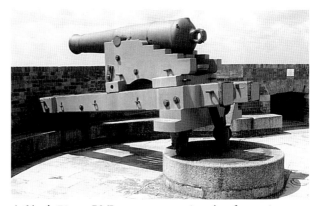

A 64-pdr 71-cwt RML gun on a rear pivot dwarf traversing platform. Two guns of this type were mounted in the practice battery at Ned's Point, Lough Swilly.   *Author*

Armstrong's 7-inch (177-mm) RBL guns of 72 cwt and 82 cwt were used in major fortresses. A number were mounted in the new forts built to defend Portsmouth and one was even mounted on Martello tower No 28 at Rye in Sussex. It soon became clear, however, particularly to the Royal Navy, that the Palliser converted guns were insufficiently powerful to deal with the ever-increasing thickness of armour of the new foreign ironclad warships currently under construction, many in British shipyards. New, larger and heavier rifled muzzle-loading guns were needed to defeat this threat.

The first of the new guns to be manufactured in any number was the 7-inch (177-mm) 7-ton RML followed by the 8-inch (203-mm) 9-ton gun of which only a few were produced. As the thickness and strength of armour plate increased, a new gun was required by both the Army and the Royal Navy and the result of this requirement was the 9-inch (228-mm) RML, weighing 12 tons. This gun was first produced in 1866 and its shell could penetrate 9 inches (228 mm) of iron plate at 2,400 yards (2,215 metres). This weapon was subsequently followed by the 10-inch (254-mm) RML, the 12-inch (304-mm) and eventually the 12.5-inch (317-mm) RML which weighed 38 tons. Later and larger guns were even heavier, culminating in the giant 17.72-inch (450-mm) guns of 100 tons. Two of these were sent to Malta and two to Gibraltar.

Although made obsolete by the advent of modern breech-loading quick-firing guns at the end of the century, many of the old RML guns remained in service into the early years of the twentieth century, particularly in practice batteries. However, although it was frequently proposed that some of the heavier RML guns should be mounted in the forts of the north of Ireland, none were.

The re-modelled western battery at Carrickfergus Castle showing the four 80-pdr 5-ton RML guns on dwarf traversing platforms which replaced the earlier 68-pdr SB guns. *Author*

The Royal Commission of 1859

The Treaty of Paris, which had brought the Crimean War to an end in 1856, confirmed in British eyes France's position as a serious rival as far as both trade and territory were concerned. The construction of the great modern port and naval base at Cherbourg, only 70 miles (112 km) from the English coast seemed to confirm France's expansionist tendencies. A new railway connected Cherbourg with Paris and despite the Emperor Napoleon III's entertainment of Queen Victoria and Prince Albert at its opening, the British public was convinced that Cherbourg was a dagger pointed at England's heart. In addition, violent anti-British feeling had recently been aroused in France by the 'Orsini Affair', when an Italian attempted to assassinate Napoleon III with bombs manufactured in England. Here, then, were further grounds for British fear of the resurgent French.

In 1856 the War Office requested a 'General Report upon the Defences of the Commercial Harbours in the United Kingdom'. The report categorised all UK ports into first, second or third class ports. In Ireland the only first class ports were Dublin, Cork, Belfast and Londonderry. The report recognised the feeble defences of Carrickfergus Castle and proposed to revise the armament of the castle and to establish a battery for four heavy guns at Grey Point on the southern shore of Belfast Lough. In addition, it was suggested that another battery for three guns should be sited on the long spit of sand south of the small town of Holywood, also on the southern shore of the lough.[3] Londonderry, on the other hand, was considered to be adequately protected by the existing defences of Lough

Foyle, though a small battery on Culmore Point was considered advisable.[4]

Interestingly the report also suggested that defences should be provided for a number of other Irish ports which were currently undefended and these were lumped together under the heading 'Second and Third Class Ports'. A battery of four guns was proposed for the defence of Larne and batteries, each of six guns, for the entrances to Strangford Lough and Carlingford Lough. While the defence of the latter location is understandable since it provided access to the prosperous town of Newry, the proposal to defend the entrance to Strangford Lough is more puzzling. This lough is comparatively shallow with hundreds of small islands making navigation hazardous, so it would seem most unlikely that a potential enemy would ever have considered it a suitable location to land troops. Nor was there much in the way of commercial shipping which might have been attacked by a raider.

By 1859 anti-French feeling in Britain had reached fever pitch and a series of leading articles were published in *The Times* and speeches made in Parliament which emphasised the parlous state of British defences. This quickly developed into a full-blown political crisis and Palmerston, the Liberal Prime Minister of the day, was forced to set up a Royal Commission to consider the defences of the United Kingdom. The commission reported in 1860 with the alarming conclusion that it might be impossible to prevent an invasion since with the advent of the steamship an enemy could concentrate an invasion force and land an

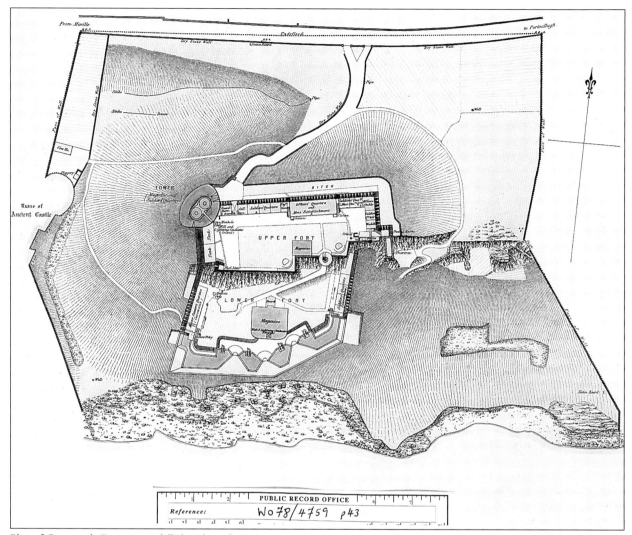

Plan of Greencastle Fort as remodelled in the early 1860s.   *PRO WO 78/4759*

army in a matter of hours.

The outcome of the commission's report was a vast scheme of fortification construction aimed at protecting the naval dockyards. In particular, Chatham, Portsmouth, Plymouth and Milford Haven were each to be protected from landward attack by a ring of new forts sited to ensure that should an invasion force land it would be kept out of artillery range of the dockyards. Large earth and brick forts incorporating all the latest ideas in fortress construction were proposed, each designed to withstand the fire of the heaviest guns. The government was soon to discover that fortifications on the scale planned by the commission were not to come cheaply. The first estimate of the construction costs came to nearly £11 million spread over four years.

This was too much for Mr Gladstone, then Chancellor of the Exchequer. As a result of his steadfast opposition to the whole scheme, and in order to avoid a crisis within the Liberal party, a number of proposed works were cancelled and the total cost reduced to a more acceptable figure of £6.5 million. However, this was still a huge sum to be expended on defence at that time.

The Royal Commission had been tasked to consider the defence of the main naval ports, and the only port in Ireland which had come under the commission's remit had been Cork. However, the additional defences planned for that port had been limited to improvements to the armament of Forts Camden and Carlisle at the entrance to the harbour while some additional towers were cancelled when the commission's original scheme was scaled down.

Between 1859 and 1861, while the commission considered the existing defences and the government debated the commission's conclusions and recommendations, there had been some improvements made to the northern Irish defences, probably as a result of the earlier 1856 report. At Carrickfergus Castle the wall of the outer ward south of the Grand Battery was remodelled for four heavy guns, three firing through wide splayed embrasures while the fourth was mounted on a raised platform and fired *en barbette*. Two 68-pdr SB guns and two 10-inch (254-mm) SB shell guns were mounted on traversing platforms at these positions. On the south wall of the inner ward a further two new gun positions were built for two 68-pdr SB guns and a new magazine was also built beneath this position. In addition, the whole eastern curtain wall was reinforced from the base of the wall down to the level of the beach by means of a granite plinth, so providing additional protection against naval gunfire.

Despite the 1856 report which considered the defences of Lough Swilly and Lough Foyle to be adequate, the fort at Greencastle was the only one of the forts on these two loughs to have its armament improved. Here the decision was taken to remove the 24-pdr SB guns and to remodel the main battery, reducing the number of guns from five to three. Three large splayed embrasures similar to those at Carrickfergus Castle were constructed and two new gun positions built on the upper, or barrack, level of the fort to form an upper battery. The new armament comprised four 68-pdr SB guns of 95 cwt and one 10-inch (254-mm) SB shell gun of 86 cwt. The two 24-pdr SB carronades were removed from the tower and replaced with two 5.5-inch (140-mm) SB iron howitzers.

Ten years were to elapse before another committee sat to consider the defences of the principal commercial ports and anchorages of the United Kingdom. The committee reported on 29 August 1870 but Belfast was the only port in the north of Ireland which warranted study and both Lough Swilly and Lough Foyle were excluded from consideration. The committee recommended that four heavy RML guns should be mounted at Carrickfergus Castle and mentioned what it termed 'floating defences' for the outer anchorage. The recommendation that a battery should be established, this time for four RML guns, at Grey Point near Helen's Bay re-emerged as did the proposal for a battery on North Sand Spit near Holywood. In the latter case the committee recommended that the battery should consist of three 9-inch (228-mm) RML guns.[5]

Carrickfergus Castle in the 1880s: the two 68-pdr SB guns of the South West Battery are just visible on top of the curtain wall.
Author's collection

Some members of the committee were not without reservations about the proposals for the new batteries at Belfast. With regard to the proposed fort at Grey Point, the senior Royal Artillery and Royal Engineers officers in Dublin were of the view that:

It yet remains a point for grave consideration whether any great expense should be incurred in the erection of the last-named works, bearing in mind the probability of a sufficiently powerful portion of the British Fleet being (during war) available at some not very distant part of the coast, which might be called on for its assistance in repelling an attack of magnitude.[6]

The committee appear to have noted these reservations for it recommended that the battery proposed for North Sand Spit should be the first to be erected and that the works at Carrickfergus and Grey Point should be the subject of further consideration. The committee did, however, suggest that 'torpedoes' (mines) should be stored locally to be used when necessary to obstruct the main shipping channel in Belfast Lough. It was shortly after the committee reported that the armament of Carrickfergus Castle was partially modernised and the castle received its first rifled guns when two of the 68-pdr SB guns from the western battery were replaced by two 80-pdr 5-ton RML guns.

In a subsequent memorandum, dated 19 December 1870, the committee noted that there were still a number of important commercial ports which had not been considered by the committee and which would be vulnerable in the event of war with what it termed a "naval power". Both Lough Swilly and Lough Foyle were noted as falling into this category, but despite belatedly including these ports among those which should be defended no suggestions were made regarding improvements to the existing defences. However, in 1872 there were almost 100 officers and gunners of the Royal Artillery manning the forts of Lough Swilly, Lough Foyle and Carrickfergus Castle in Belfast Lough. Captain Campbell, Lieutenant Kelly and 64 rank and file of the 21st Brigade RA were stationed in Buncrana, Greencastle Fort, Knockalla Fort and Ned's Point Fort. The remaining forts and Carrickfergus Castle were manned by four Master Gunners, one sergeant and 24 rank and file of the Coast Brigade RA, the successor unit to the old Invalid Detachment.[7]

The situation changed towards the end of the decade and by 1879 all the forts on the western shore of Lough Swilly had been virtually disarmed and only Knockalla Fort retained three guns. Two guns remained on the tower, one 18-pdr 38-cwt SB gun and one 5.5-inch (139-mm) howitzer, and a single 24-pdr SB gun on the upper battery.

Macamish Fort had been disarmed and Rathmullen Fort had been dismantled and let to a Mr Henderson who was described as a "contractor".[8]

On the Erne, Enniskillen continued to be regarded as an important strategic location guarding the only feasible crossing place between Upper and Lower Lough Erne. As late as 1875 the Defence Committee confirmed that:

> Enniskillen is an important military station, and the main barracks there are all adapted for defence. The Castle and Main Barracks stand on the island on which the town is situated, and the Redoubt Barracks, now used as a hospital, are on the other or western side of Lough Erne. Howitzers are at the four corners of the redoubt, which is square, surrounded by a ditch and in good repair.[9]

8 Breech-Loaders and Battleships 1881–1900

The 'Admiral' class battleship HMS *Benbow*. Completed in 1888, this battleship had a displacement of 10,600 tons and was armed with two huge 16.25-inch (412-mm) BL guns.

Author's collection

1881–1889

At the start of the penultimate decade of the nineteenth century, technology continued to advance in leaps and bounds while the Royal Navy and the Army vainly attempted to keep pace. By the early 1880s the period of greatest experimentation in ship design was over and the ironclad battleships were beginning to be built according to a number of proven principles. The navy had been loath to abandon full sailing rig in its ships, maintaining both sail and steam propulsion, partly through an innate conservatism but also because of the comparatively small bunker capacity of the early battleship designs. In 1873

HMS *Devastation* was launched, a mastless breastwork monitor of 9,330 tons of which 2,540 tons was armour. This coast defence ship was armed with four 12-inch (304-mm) 35-ton RML guns mounted in pairs in two turrets. She proved to be a very successful sea-going ship with an adequate endurance since she was able to carry three times the quantity of coal when compared with other battleships of the period.

Despite one or two design aberrations in the late 1870s it was HMS *Devastation* which was to prove to be the pattern for battleships of the future. By 1879 HMS

Dreadnought, another mastless battleship, was in commission, to be followed four years later by HMS *Collingwood*, the first of six 'Admiral' class battleships. These latter ships were very similar to HMS *Devastation* but had a higher freeboard (height of deck above sea) fore and aft. However, the one great difference between the 'Admirals' and HMS *Devastation* lay in the armament. Whereas HMS *Devastation* was armed with four large RML guns, the 'Admirals' mounted four breech-loading 12-inch (304-mm) 45-ton guns on barbette mountings. In addition they each had a secondary battery in the superstructure and machine guns in the two fighting tops on the single pole mast.

The Royal Navy, while struggling to combine effectively steam propulsion, armour and fuel capacity in the design of its new ships, was also faced with the rapidly developing problem of arming them with suitable guns. The problem lay in achieving sufficient muzzle velocity to enable a shell to penetrate the ever-increasing thickness of armour being fitted to the new battleships being built for European navies. The failure of shells from Armstrong's 7-inch (177-mm) RBL gun to penetrate any real thickness of armour had led to the reversion to the use of muzzle-loading guns.

The muzzle-loading guns themselves were becoming ever larger as their designers endeavoured to improve their capability to penetrate armour but the designers were up against a new problem. As the guns became larger the length of the chase was restricted by the problem of loading the gun. In the larger battleships this problem was partially overcome by a system of loading where the barrel was lowered to enable the gun to be loaded hydraulically through an aperture in the deck in front of the turret. This meant that loading the guns became a slow procedure and also potentially dangerous because there was always the possibility of loading a second charge and shell on top of a misfire, as happened in HMS *Thunderer* in 1879.

It was this slow rate of fire which was becoming the main limitation in the use of muzzle-loading guns for coast defence. Research into steam engines was resulting in ever more powerful engines which, when linked to twin screws, were propelling warships at much increased speeds. With ships capable of 15–16 knots, guns in armoured casemates could only fire one or two rounds before the target had moved out of the limited field of traverse of the gun. This was particularly the case when trying to engage the new torpedo boats now coming into service, many of which had a speed approaching 20 knots. Breech-loading guns had a much faster rate of fire when compared with muzzle-loaders, while the new, small quick-firing guns which used

A 6-inch (152-mm) BL gun on a hydro-pneumatic mounting, in the raised position. Similar guns were subsequently mounted in Inch and Ned's Point Forts.

Author's collection

fixed round ammunition, where the shell was attached to a brass cartridge case containing the propelling charge and igniter, had an even faster rate of fire. So it was becoming clear that breech-loading and quick-firing guns were to be the weapons of the future.

At this time experiments were being carried out in the use of slow-burning gun powder as the propellant for guns. When compared with the standard powder used in charges at that time, the new slow-burning powder expended much less energy in the initial explosion, so producing higher muzzle velocities. However, to obtain the full effect of this slower combustion a gun with a much longer bore was required. Since muzzle-loading guns mounted in both casemates and turrets tended to have a limitation on the overall length of the gun, it was almost impossible to take full advantage of this new development.

A gun mounted in an open gun pit firing *en barbette* could be traversed over a greater arc than one installed in an armoured casemate. An open gun pit was also vastly cheaper to construct but there still remained the problem that when loading a RML gun the gun crew would be exposed to enemy fire. This problem had been addressed by Captain Moncreiff, an officer of the Edinburgh Artillery Militia, who designed a counter-weight mounting which enabled guns to be loaded by the crew within the gun pit. The gun was raised to fire by releasing the counterweight and then, when the gun fired, the recoil forced the weight upwards again and the barrel sank down into the gun pit ready for re-loading. A number of these mountings were taken into service, particularly in the land forts protecting Portsmouth, Plymouth and Milford Haven but they were not popular with the War Office. These mountings were mainly used with 64-pdr RML and 7-inch (177-mm) RBL guns but did not prove successful with the larger RMLs.

By the mid-1880s Armstrong had successfully overcome the problems with the breech-locking problem inherent in his earlier designs, and with the advent of reliable breech-loading guns it became necessary to ensure maximum use was made of their improved rate of fire. This precluded the use of the guns in armoured casemates which would limit their arc of traverse, so the guns were mounted in open gun pits. Strangely, the War Office was still worried about protection for the gun crews despite the fact that a single gun in a gun pit offered a very small target to the enemy ship engaging it. The difficulty in engaging such a target for a ship was compounded by the instability of the gun platform which the ship provided. To satisfy the War Office, the Elswick Ordnance Company developed a new 'disappearing' mounting for 6-inch (152-mm), 8-inch (203-mm) and 10-inch (254-mm) BL guns using a hydro-pneumatic system. This mounting enabled the gun to be loaded within the pit and then raised in the same way as the older Moncreiff system but, unlike the latter, it could be used successfully with these much larger guns. An armoured shield covered the top of the gun pit through which the gun was raised to its firing position and this provided additional protection for the gun crew.

The hydro-pneumatic mounting was adopted by the War Office and used in a number of locations, particularly overseas. Once again, however, there were a number of problems associated with this form of mounting. The rate of fire was slower than if the gun was mounted *en barbette* since it had to be raised and lowered between each round fired. Also the maximum range of the gun was constrained because no carriage could be developed to elevate the gun beyond an angle of 20 degrees. At the end of the nineteenth century this was not a major drawback but with the turn of the century came the development of the new all-big-gun 'Dreadnought' battleships. These ships were armed with 12-inch (304-mm) and 13.5-inch (343-mm) BL guns and so increased range became essential if coastal defence guns were to be able to engage these ships effectively.

All these technological developments meant that from 1859 onwards the Admiralty and the War Office were constantly endeavouring to improve the defences of the major naval bases from attack by enemy ironclads. Consideration of the defences of the naval ports only served to emphasise how defenceless the major commercial ports of the United Kingdom were. Most of these ports still relied on the old defences constructed during the Napoleonic War, with a few batteries added as a result of the Royal Commission of 1859.

In 1882 the Morley Committee sat to consider the defence of the commercial harbours of the United Kingdom. The committee stated that:

. . . they refrain from recommending works for the defence of minor harbours because they are impressed with the necessity of rendering the larger mercantile harbours, as far as possible, secure from attack, before any attempt is made to protect places of secondary importance'.[1]

In Ireland the committee only considered Dublin and Belfast and for the latter it recommended two self-defensible batteries: the first for two 10-inch (254-mm) RML guns in a position west of Carrickfergus; and a second for four 10-inch (254-mm) and two 64-pdr RML guns on a site 1,000 yards (923 metres) west of Grey Point on the southern shore of the Belfast Lough. A third battery for three 7-inch (177-mm) 6.5-ton RBL guns was proposed to be sited on the water's edge at Holywood to command the narrow channel and entrance leading to Belfast docks. The existing armament of Carrickfergus Castle, which at that date comprised two 80-pdr 5-ton RML guns and four 68-pdr SB guns was to be changed to six 64-pdr RMLs. Finally, the committee recommended that a small quota of submarine mines should be held ready to be placed at or near the entrance to the narrow channel.[2]

Neither Lough Swilly nor Lough Foyle were considered by the Morley Committee since both were obviously places of secondary importance. However, in the same year the GOC Ireland, General HSH Prince Edward of Saxe-Weimar, drew attention to the uselessness of the defences of both loughs in their current condition but he was not prepared to see these defences given up. He directed the senior Royal Artillery and Royal Engineers officers in Dublin to report on the defences. The view of the GOC Royal Artillery was that Greencastle Fort was difficult and dangerous to fight because of the wall of rock immediately behind the lower battery but the Commander Royal Engineers believed that there was sufficient room to erect substantial cover for the men manning the guns. General Saxe-Weimar believed that this protective cover should be built as soon as possible and that the smooth-bore guns replaced by an equal number of 64-pdr 71-cwt RML guns. Both officers recommended the retention of Ned's Point Fort at Buncrana and Inch Fort. However, the Adjutant General, Lord Wolseley, did not support this proposal.[3]

The matter was referred to the Admiralty in August 1883

The Upper battery at Greencastle Fort: the picture shows the fort after conversion to a hotel, but one of the Upper battery gun positions can still be seen in the centre of the picture.

Author's collection

for their answers to two questions: firstly, whether it was of importance to the Royal Navy that either or both of the loughs in question should be made secure anchorages in time of war; and secondly, whether such anchorages should be made safe against the attack of ironclads or only against unarmoured cruisers. Their Lordships replied that it would be desirable to improve the defences of Lough Foyle but they did not consider it important that the lough should "be protected against the entrance of ironclads or that defensive works should be constructed for the purpose of protecting the anchorage of Lough Swilly".[4]

The proposed defences of the loughs were considered again in November 1884 when the Defence Committee decided on the rearming of Greencastle Fort with three 7-inch (177-mm) RBL guns and the construction of a battery on Magilligan Point for three similar guns. The following year the Defence Committee agreed the transfer of three 7-inch (177-mm) RBL guns on counterweight carriages from Fort Hubberstone in Milford Haven to Lough Foyle. These guns were destined to arm the new battery on Magilligan Point as the counter-weight carriages were considered particularly suitable for positions in low-lying ground.[5] This decision was never acted upon and the armament of the Lough Foyle defences remained unchanged.

In 1885 the whole matter of advising on the defence of ports and harbours became the responsibility of a new committee, the RA and RE Works Committee, which reported directly to the Defence Committee. This new committee visited Lough Swilly and Lough Foyle and recommended that the defences of the former should be dismantled except for Ned's Point Fort. This was to be

retained as a practice battery with an armament of two 64-pdr RML guns and two 24-pdr 50-cwt SB guns. As regards Lough Foyle, the proposals for the installation of the RBL guns appear to have been dropped. Instead it was suggested that Magilligan Tower should be re-armed with one 64-pdr RML gun and that a slight alteration should be made to the upper battery of Greencastle Fort to permit the left-hand gun to fire seawards.[6]

Two years earlier, in 1883, Knockalla Fort had been finally disarmed. In October the Surveyor General of Ordnance, in accordance with a suggestion from the Director of Artillery, approved the disposal of the seven old cast-iron guns from the *Hoche*. Since the cost of removing the guns to Woolwich was more than they were worth as trophies, they were to be sold as old iron after being rendered unserviceable. So, after probably 100 years of service these guns came to an ignominious end.

Five years then elapsed and in that time the defences of Lough Swilly were effectively dismantled, with the exception of Ned's Point Fort. On Lough Foyle none of the recommended changes were carried out to Greencastle Fort, and Magilligan Tower was not re-armed.

At this time the defence of Belfast was considered altogether more important than either Lough Swilly or Lough Foyle. Belfast was developing extremely rapidly during this period in its history and becoming a prosperous manufacturing city. Indeed, by 1901 Belfast was a city of 349,180 people compared with 87,062 in 1852; its linen mills were famous worldwide and the Belfast Ropeworks Company was amongst the largest in the world. Even more important as far as the Admiralty was concerned, it possessed a large shipbuilding and ship-repairing industry. In a memorandum entitled 'The Revision of Armaments – Belfast', dated 4 July 1888, the RA and RE Works Committee deemed the defence of Belfast necessary "to protect vessels seeking shelter from pursuit, protecting the anchorage of Carrickfergus and denying the use of it to an enemy". The committee believed such defence would "serve to inspire the inhabitants of this important place with confidence".[7] The committee proposed the construction of two batteries for breech-loading guns: one at Kilroot on the northern shore of Belfast Lough, three miles (5 km) beyond Carrickfergus; and the other almost opposite, across the lough at Grey Point in County Down, the same location favoured by the 1870 committee for a battery of four heavy RML guns.

The committee recommended an armament of three 6-inch (152-mm) BL guns for Kilroot and two similar guns for Grey Point. These guns were to be mounted on the new

The Antrim Artillery pictured at repository drill on the drill ground at Carrickfergus Castle. The photograph shows training being carried out in the 1880s with 64-pdr RML guns. The gun on the far right appears to be a 20-pdr RBL gun on an iron garrison carriage.
Author's collection

hydro-pneumatic (HP) mountings. In addition, Grey Point was to have a second battery of four 9-inch (228-mm) RML guns on long-range mountings.[8]

The decision to defend Belfast Lough with modern weapons meant that Carrickfergus Castle was no longer required as a coast defence fortification. However, the committee proposed that the existing armament should be retained for drill purposes for the training of the Antrim Royal Garrison Artillery. It was also at this time that the decision was taken to allocate submarine mining stores to Belfast and Dublin, but not the actual mines. The stores were sufficient for a minefield of 61 mines to close the narrow shipping channel leading into Belfast. The plan to use submarine mines was short lived, for by 1895 the Joint Naval and Military Committee recommended that the minefields be withdrawn.

1889–1900

In 1889 there was a complete volte face on the part of the Admiralty with regard to its view of the value of Lough Swilly to the Royal Navy. Rear Admiral Sir George Tryon RN wrote to the Defence Committee pointing out that in any modern war, particularly one with France, the shipping routes north and south of Ireland could be very vulnerable to attack. There was a vital need for two strategic harbours of refuge in Ireland and he suggested Berehaven in the south-west and Lough Swilly in the north-west were the most suitable. He favoured Lough Swilly over Lough Foyle because the navigation in the former was simpler. In July 1889 the RA and RE Works Committee visited Lough Swilly and recommended that the defence of that lough ought to take precedence over Berehaven. In its report the

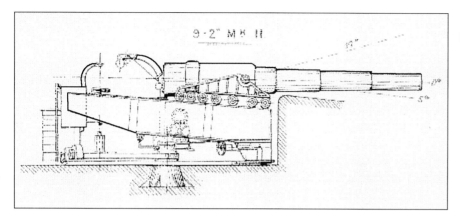

Drawing of a 9.2-inch (233-mm) BL gun on a Mk II mounting.

Author's collection

committee stated:

> Lough Swilly . . . occupies a unique position on the north coast, towards which it must be remembered much of the trade which now passes by the south would probably be directed in time of war, and there is no fortified port in the neighbourhood. Lough Swilly, defended, would not only serve the purpose of a harbour of refuge for merchant ships, but, being within 80 miles [128 km] of the Mull of Cantyre [sic] and the North Channel, which at that point is only 13 miles [20.8 km] wide, it would have an important bearing on the defence of the ports lying within St George's Channel and the Irish Sea especially Belfast, the Clyde and Liverpool.[10]

The committee had little to say about Lough Foyle, feeling that there was no comparison between it and Lough Swilly as a harbour of refuge. Indeed, had it not been for the trade with Londonderry it was felt that Lough Foyle would be of no importance whatsoever and so the committee did not recommend improving Greencastle Fort. All their recommendations related to Lough Swilly and involved the modernisation of the defence works on the eastern shore which the committee considered was more accessible, particularly since there was a railway running from Londonderry to Buncrana. The committee also believed that with the increased ranges of modern weapons there was no longer a need to have forts on both sides of the lough.

The outcome of the committee's visit was the proposal, ratified by the Defence Committee in 1890, that Dunree Fort should be re-armed with breech-loading and quick-firing guns. Two 4.7-inch (120-mm) QF guns were to be mounted in the old fort itself, one on the main battery and the other on the tower, while two 6-inch (152-mm) BL guns on HP mountings were to be sited behind the fort, one on either side of the new lighthouse. For local defence two 3-pdr QF guns on field carriages were to be

provided and Ned's Point Fort was also to be re-armed but with three of the older 7-inch (177-mm) RBL guns.

The 4.7-inch (120-mm) QF gun was selected for use against the new torpedo boats and torpedo-boat destroyers coming into service at that time, many of which now had a speed approaching 25 knots. For the anti-torpedo boat role a quick-firing gun of sufficiently large calibre to enable it to fire a heavy shell was required. Neither the 6-pdr QF gun or the larger 12-pdr QF fired a shell heavy enough to damage seriously these fast and agile ships. So the preferred weapon for this role was now the 4.7-inch (120-mm) QF gun which fired a shell weighing 45 lbs (20 kg). Although termed a quick-firer, the 4.7 in gun fired separate-loading ammunition with the shell being loaded first, followed by the brass cartridge case, but the rate of fire was still considerably faster than the breech-loaders using 'bagged' charges.

The following year, 1891, the Defence Committee once again emphasised the importance of Lough Swilly from the naval point of view and directed the RA and RE Works Committee to prepare a further report with a view to providing a new battery mounting the heavier 9.2-inch (233-mm) BL guns. The latter committee rejected Dunaff and Fanad Heads at the mouth of the lough as being too inaccessible and decided on Lenan Head, five miles (8 km) north of Dunree Fort, as the site for the new battery. The proposed armament for this new battery was to include one 9.2-inch (233-mm) Mk I BL gun supported by two 9-inch (228-mm) RML guns on long-range mountings. This modern breech-loading gun fired a shell weighing 380 lbs (173 kg) to a maximum range of 15,000 yards (13,846 metres), but was still mounted on an old pattern carriage which recoiled up the inclined plane of the slide on a traversing platform which itself had scarcely changed in 100 years.

The role of the 9.2 in gun was to cover an arc of 180

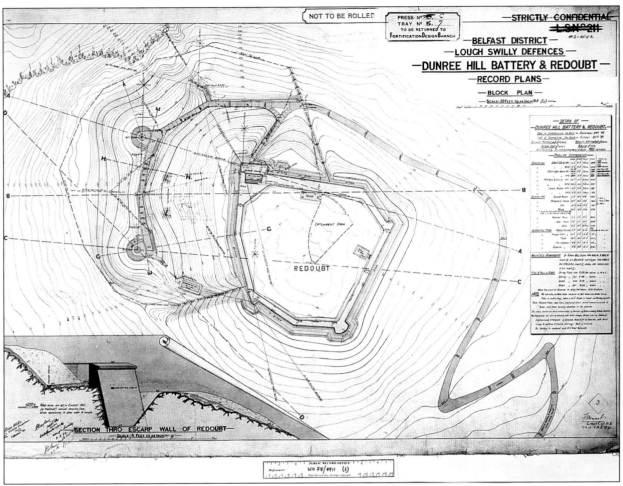

Plan of Dunree Redoubt and battery, 1899.

degrees from Dunaff Head on the right of the arc to Dunree on the left, and its fire was designed to cross with that of the guns of Dunree. The fire of the two RMLs was to cover the same area of water but would also be of "especial value should an enemy vessel attempt to anchor under the shelter of either head".[11] The battery was also to be provided with two 6-pdr QF guns on cone mountings to defend the possible landing places in Lenan Bay and Dunaff Port and also three machine-guns on field carriages for landward defence.

While the new battery at Lenan was the most important recommendation to be made by the committee, the armament of the remaining forts on the eastern shore was considered and amended. The committee reconsidered their earlier proposal for Dunree Fort, substituting one 6-inch (152-mm) BL gun on an HP mounting for the 4.7-inch (120-mm) gun planned for the main battery in the old fort. A single 6-pdr QF gun on a cone mounting was substituted for the 4.7-inch (120-mm) gun proposed for the tower. The location of the two 6-inch (152-mm) guns planned to be sited near the lighthouse was also changed, a position further up Dunree Hill being selected instead, and the gun mountings changed from hydro-pneumatic to *en barbette*.

The committee also decided that Ned's Point and Inch forts should be each re-armed with two 9-inch (228-mm) RML guns on long-range mountings. In their report they emphasised the value of Lough Swilly as a practice range, saying:

The Committee wish to draw attention to the unusual facilities for practice Lough Swilly offers. There is so little traffic of any kind, that a clear range can always be maintained, and if the armaments which we propose were mounted there would be opportunities of

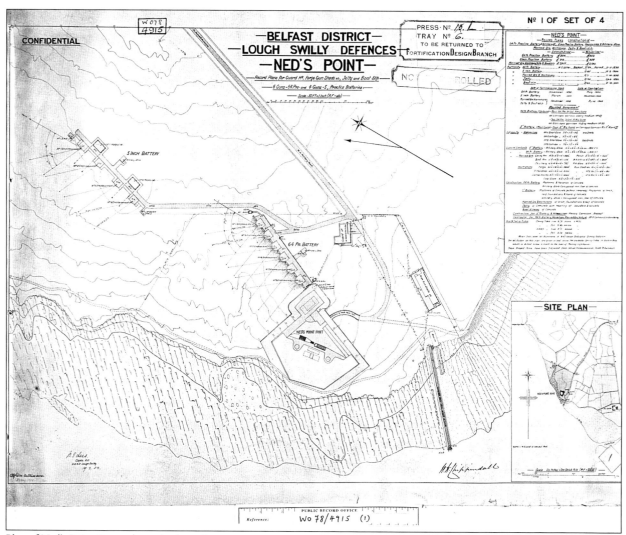

Plan of Ned's Point Fort and practice batteries.

PRO WO 78/4915

practising with 9.2 in BL, 6 in BL and 9 in RML guns at stationary or moving targets, with or without assistance of PF, such as rarely occurs in the more or less frequented waters of ports of the United Kingdom.[12]

With a constant stream of differing recommendations emanating from the various committees in the early 1890s it is, perhaps, not surprising that the authorities were somewhat loath to act immediately on these recommendations. In 1893 the recommended main armament of Lenan Fort was changed to three 9.2-inch (233-mm) BL guns while the secondary armament of two 6-pdr QF guns was to be retained. In 1895 the RA and RE Works Committee met to consider a revision of the armaments for the coastal defences of the United

Kingdom involving the substitution of BL and QF guns for the heavy and medium RMLs in place. Once again the proposed armament of the forts in the north of Ireland was to change.

Lenan Fort retained a main armament of three 9.2-inch (233-mm) BL guns, two Mk Is and a Mk IV, but the 6-pdr QF guns were no longer approved and were to be replaced by three additional machine-guns. The role of the main armament at Lenan was to defend the anchorage against attack by battleships or heavy armoured cruisers while the 6-inch (152-mm) guns at Dunree were to provide the close defence of the entrance to the lough.

At Dunree the committee proposed the remodelling of the old fort to enable it to mount two 4.7-inch (120-mm)

Inch Fort: the picture shows the interior of the fort with one of the 6-inch (152-mm) HP gun positions in the background.

Author

The interior of Ned's Point Fort, Buncrana, showing the entrance to the magazine.
Author

Mk IV QF guns. The remodelling involved filling in the main battery terreplein, building two concrete gun positions for the new QF guns with magazines below, and demolishing the Martello tower and all the old buildings within the fort. A depression rangefinder and a chart house were to be sited where the old tower had been. Work commenced on the old fort in October 1894 and was completed three years later at a cost of £2,034 10s.

Work on the upper battery at Dunree commenced in 1895 after additional land had been purchased from the local landowner, Major Charles Bateson Harvey. The two new gun positions and magazines for the proposed battery of two 6-inch (152-mm) Mk IV BL guns were sited about two-thirds of the way up the hill. At the same time the crest of Dunree Hill, which had always been a problem for the defenders of the old fort, was fortified with a concrete redoubt roughly pentagonal in shape. The redoubt was surrounded by a ditch that was defended on the south-eastern side by a bastion and on the south-western and eastern sides by two demi-bastions. The redoubt contained a catchment area for rainwater to supply the fort and barrack accommodation and a guard room, and there were two depression rangefinders, one mounted on the roof of the guard room and one on the redoubt wall. Below the redoubt the gun positions and magazines were surrounded by an 'unclimbable' steel palisade. The cost of the battery and redoubt came to £10,323, which was £239 less than the original estimated cost.

At Ned's Point Fort, outside Buncrana, and Inch Fort, opposite Rathmullen, the committee recommended that the proposed RML guns should be replaced by two 6-inch (152-mm) guns on HP mountings in each fort. In, addition the two 64-pdr RML guns should be retained at Ned's Point for drill purposes. At both these old forts the main battery terrepleins were filled in with earth into which two deep concrete gun pits were sunk for the HP mountings for the new guns. At Ned's Point the upper storey of the defensible guard house was removed and a depression rangefinder mounted on the top. This work was complete by 1897.

Of the three forts on the eastern shore the one that most lent itself to modernisation was Inch Fort. The natural rock of the cliff on which the fort was sited acted as the scarp of the battery. With the Martello tower reduced in height so that no part of it was visible from the sea, the location of the fort could not be easily identified by attacking warships. The armament of two 6-inch (152-mm) guns on HP mountings was ideal as no part of the gun was visible except for a period of about ten seconds when it was raised and fired. The southern and western sides were protected by a ditch and on the western side the ditch was defended by a demi-caponier entered by way of a tunnel from the No 2 gun position. In the ten years that the modernised Inch Fort was part of the defences of Lough Swilly it and the fort at Ned's Point were manned by two companies of the Londonderry Artillery Militia.

Having considered Lough Swilly, the RA and RE Works Committee turned its attention to Belfast Lough. At Kilroot the armament of the new battery which had been proposed in 1888 was reduced by one 6-inch (152-mm) gun while at Grey Point the proposed battery of four heavy RML guns on long-range mountings was also deleted. Three machine-guns were to be provided for each battery for local defence. The armament of Carrickfergus Castle, which by this date comprised four 80-pdr 5-ton RML and two 68-pdr SB guns, was retained for drill purposes only.

The Approach of War 1900–1914

9

Work on Lenan Fort commenced in 1901 and was complete by October 1902. The fort comprised three concrete gun positions on the cliff edge facing north with magazines, stores, barrack accommodation and a guard house. The centre and left gun positions were linked by a sunken road running from the centre of the fort while the right-hand position was approached along a separate sunken road. The centre and right-hand positions were built over an underground magazine containing cartridge and shell stores and a gun crew shelter which served both guns, but the left-hand position had its own separate magazine and shelter. Each gun had its own depression

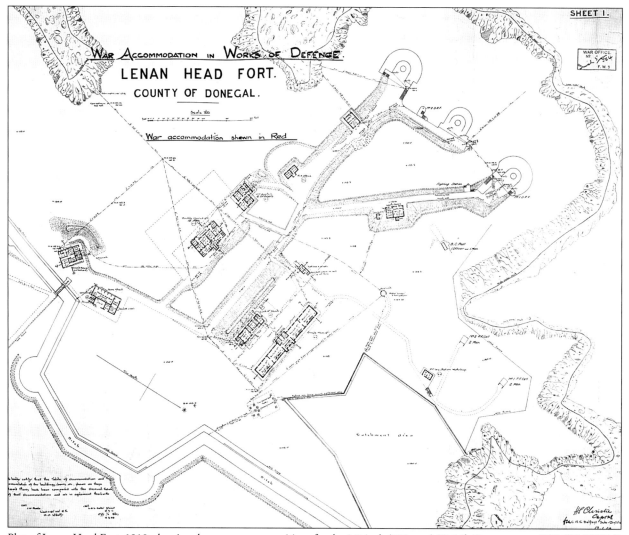

Plan of Lenan Head Fort, 1910, showing the two new gun positions for the 9.2-inch (233-mm) BL Mk X guns. *PRO WO 78/4748*

Ned's Point 64-pdr RML practice battery position: in the foreground is the 'C' pivot for one of the 64-pdr 71-cwt RML guns.   *Author*

rangefinder with one position sited between the centre and left emplacements and the other two mounted on the concrete parapets of the centre and right gun positions. Some 50 yards (45 metres) behind the right-hand gun was the battery commander's post and a further 75 yards (70 metres) behind it there were two position finding cells sunk into the ground and protected by concrete roofs.

When first completed there was accommodation for a married warrant officer and three other married NCOs or gunners, together with an accommodation block for 56 single gunners. In 1911 the census showed a garrison totalling 28 of all ranks occupying the fort. Under war conditions, however, the double married quarters building was to provide accommodation for an additional 18 gunners while the warrant officer's quarter was to be used to accommodate six officers.

Providing the main defence for the fort on the northern side were the sheer cliffs dropping down to the sea, while across the base of the small peninsula on which the fort was sited a ditch was dug. This ditch was 25 feet (7.6 metres) wide and 15 feet (4.6 metres) deep with a concrete scarp. Halfway along its length it projected out and away from the main accommodation area of the fort forming a D-shaped salient but no caponiers were provided to defend it. Entrance to the fort was across a drawbridge and on the landward side the fort was surrounded by a five-strand barbed wire fence. The total cost of the construction of the fort was £25,031.

Earlier comments by the RA and RE Works Committee concerning the suitability of Lough Swilly for firing practice had not fallen on deaf ears. In 1898 work had started on two practice batteries sited just outside the

walls of Ned's Point Fort. The first battery, consisting of a low concrete wall and concrete bases for six traversing platforms, was for two 64-pdr RML 71-cwt guns on 'C' pivots and four 64-pdr RML 64-cwt guns on 'A' pivots. Cartridge recesses were provided between each gun position and a small magazine was built to the rear of the battery. At each end of the battery there was a position for a depression rangefinder. The battery was completed in 1900 but by then the decision had been taken to increase the practice facilities by constructing a second battery position for four 5-inch (127-mm) BL guns, with a magazine and positions for two depression rangefinders. These were ex-naval guns which had been removed from ships and replaced by the new 4.7-inch (120-mm) QF and 6-inch (152-mm) QF guns. The old 5-inch (127-mm)BLs were then transferred to practice batteries replacing the obsolete 64-pdrs.[1]

The second battery was built to a very simple design comprising four concrete ground platforms without the low concrete wall. The work took only eight months to complete and the contractors were Messrs Campbell and Son of Belfast, the same firm that had been responsible for the modernisation of Inch Fort. The contractor for the 64-pdr battery was Robert Colhoun of Londonderry. Both batteries provided training facilities for the 15th Company RGA, which had been stationed in Londonderry since 1902, the Donegal Artillery Militia and the Londonderry Artillery Militia.

At Carrickfergus Castle, improvements in the guns of the practice battery were also proposed. In 1898 four 7-inch 6.5-ton RML guns were approved for the castle, with two to be mounted on the practice ground and two on the south-east wall of the castle. These guns were never mounted but 18 months later, in February 1902, two 5-inch (127-mm) BL guns were approved for the practice battery. It would appear that these guns were actually installed as the remains of the mountings can still be seen today above the beach, below the east side of the gatehouse, alongside a C-pivot for a 64-pdr RML gun.[2]

The Belfast District Defence Scheme (revised to 1 January 1904) defined the threat to Lough Swilly as being from attack by several armoured cruisers and also attack by 2nd Class torpedo boats, that is torpedo boats carried close to the target and then launched from a 'mother' ship.[3] For Belfast the defences were designed to prevent an enemy cruiser entering the lough and to defeat an attack by 2nd Class torpedo boats. The defence plan noted that the Lough Swilly defences were completely armed for the first time and the Lough Swilly Fortress, which included the whole of the Innishowen Peninsula and the peninsula between Lough Swilly and Mulroy Bay, was now established.

The old fort at Knockalla was selected as the station for the naval officer responsible for the regulation of traffic and the Port War Signal Station was established at Fanad Head. This was somewhat surprising as both were on the western shore of the lough with all the problems of communication that this entailed. The 4.7-inch (120-mm) QF battery at Dunree Fort was designated the examination battery with the role of supporting the Royal Navy examination steamers which inspected shipping entering the lough and a fixed beam searchlight was provided to illuminate the area of water in front of the fort. A second emplacement for a movable searchlight was in course of construction below the fort while on a patch of flat ground below the battery on Dunree Hill a new practice battery was built. This was a four-gun battery with two 6-inch (152-mm) Mk IV BL guns and two 5-inch (127-mm) BL guns. In 1903 a new shed and store for the movable armament of three machine-guns was built to replace one that had been destroyed by fire earlier in the year.

By 1905 it was becoming clear to British policy makers that the major threat to Britain's naval supremacy and, therefore, Britain's interests worldwide was no longer France but Germany. In Germany the First Navy Law providing for a six-year programme for the construction of 12 new battleships had been passed by the Reichstag in 1898. In 1900 the Reichstag passed the Second Navy Law doubling the number of battleships to be built and the naval race between Britain and Germany was truly on.

To the British politicians it was clear that Britain needed a major ally on the Continent to counter balance the Triple Alliance of Germany, Austria-Hungary and Italy. In 1904 Britain and France signed the Entente Cordiale and, although the Entente was not a military alliance, it ensured that British military planners now accepted that France was an ally rather than a potential enemy. At a stroke, areas of the United Kingdom which the planners previously believed threatened in a war with France no longer were. Instead, other areas, particularly along the eastern coasts of England and Scotland, which had never seemed vulnerable when France was considered the major threat, were now obviously open to attack by Germany.

In the same year, 1905, the Admiralty and the War Office set up a joint committee with instructions to

A 9.2-inch (233-mm) BL Mk X gun: the gun is of the same type as the two guns installed at Lenan Head Fort in 1910.

Author's collection

"report what additions or alterations, if any, are necessary to the existing fixed defences of all defended ports at home to suit modern conditions".[4] The committee was under the presidency of General JF Owen with four other members, two each from the Army and the Royal Navy. This committee, which was to have great influence on future policy concerning fixed defences in the United Kingdom and overseas, became known as the Owen Committee.

The Owen Committee took as the basis for its considerations the fact that the ports of the United Kingdom might be subjected to three classes of naval attack. These were: Class A – Attack by Battleships; Class B – Attack by Armoured Cruisers; and Class C – Attack by Unarmoured Cruisers, Torpedo Boats or Block Ships.

Only the major naval ports were considered likely to be attacked by battleships and since none of these were in Ireland the highest level of threat the island was likely to incur was considered to be Class B attack. The only ports and harbours in Ireland considered to be likely to be subjected to such attack were Cork, Berehaven and Lough Swilly, all used by the Royal Navy. The threat of attack on Belfast, a purely commercial port, was determined to be Class C.

The committee also rationalised the types of armament it considered should be provided to defend the ports and harbours against each type of attack. For defence against Class A and Class B attack two types of gun were considered: the 9.2-inch (233-mm) BL gun and the 12-inch (304-mm) BL gun. By 1905 the latest marks of the 9.2-inch (233-mm) gun were the Marks IX and X, both of which, on a mounting which permitted 15 degrees of elevation, fired a shell weighing 380 lbs (172 kg) to a range of 17,500 yards (16,153 metres). Having considered the 9.2-inch (233-mm) and 12-inch (304-mm) BL guns the committee felt that the angles of elevation and descent of shells from each gun did not differ sufficiently to affect long-range shooting, but in barrel life and rapidity of fire the 9.2-inch (233-mm) gun was greatly superior.[5] In these circumstances the committee did not believe the mounting of any other nature of gun than the 9.2-inch (233mm) BL gun was necessary in order to deter attacks by battleships or armoured cruisers. The committee then turned its attention to attack by unarmoured ships (Class C). Here the requirement was for rapidity of fire combined with as great a weight of shell as could be provided. The committee recommended the 6-inch (152-mm) BL Mk VII gun and the 4.7-inch (120-mm) QF Mk V gun as being the most appropriate for this role.

Having laid down the types of attacks to be defended against and the most appropriate guns to meet such attacks, the committee then considered all the naval ports and commercial ports and harbours in the United Kingdom, recommending changes in the armament as necessary. For Lough Swilly the recommendations were the removal of the three obsolescent 9.2-inch (233-mm) guns at Lenan Fort and in their place two of the new Mk X guns were to be installed. At Dunree the two old pattern 6-inch (152-mm) BL Mk VI guns, which had replaced the original Mk IV guns in 1904, were to be replaced with two of the latest Mk VII guns and the two 4.7-inch (120-mm) QF guns were to be removed from the fort. With the introduction of the more powerful guns at Lenan and Dunree forts there was no longer any need to retain Ned's Point and Inch forts in service and both were to be abandoned and their armament removed.

At Belfast the committee was satisfied that the new forts planned and in course of construction provided adequate defence against Class C attack and so no changes were recommended. The provision of electric lights (searchlights) at all ports was part of the committee's remit but, interestingly, no electric lights were considered necessary for the defence of Belfast Lough.

The recommendations of the Owen Committee were not acted upon immediately. In 1906 the Londonderry Defence Scheme was virtually unchanged from the scheme of two years before but a number of machine-guns were now to be provided as a movable armament for the general defence of the forts. The thinking at this time

This picture shows two of the 9.2-inch (233-mm) BL gun positions at Lenan Head Fort. In the foreground is one of the original gun positions while behind is one of the positions for the newer Mk X guns installed in 1910. *Author*

was that the provision of machine-guns reduced the size of the infantry force needed to defend the forts in time of war. A total of 13 machine-guns were now on the establishment of the four forts, and sheds were provided at each for the guns and the storage of ammunition. Lenan Fort had the largest number of guns with six .303-inch (7.6-mm) Gardner guns on Mk I infantry carriages, while Dunree Fort had three and Ned's Point Fort two .303-inch (7.6-mm) Maxim machine-guns respectively, also on infantry carriages. Only Inch Fort differed and here there were two .303-inch (7.6-mm) Gardner guns but these were fixed on parapet mountings. The Lough Swilly forts were still manned by 15th Company RGA and by elements of the Antrim Artillery Militia from Carrickfergus, but the garrisons of Ned's Point and Inch were now provided by one company of the Londonderry Artillery Militia rather than two as in 1904.[6]

It was not until 1911 that the guns at Lenan were replaced by two more powerful Mk X guns. The replacement of the guns involved constructing two larger gun positions for the new guns and the two existing flank gun pits were chosen for modification. By 1909 the fort was armed with only two guns: the Mark IV and one of the Mark Is as the second Mark I with its barbette mounting had been removed to store in Londonderry. The two guns were removed by 15th Company RGA and replaced by two new Mark X guns which had been brought to Lenan by sea. The work at the fort took place between September 1909 and the early months of 1911, by which time the new guns were operational but the old guns, one unserviceable and one obsolete, were not removed from Lenan to Woolwich until May 1914.[7]

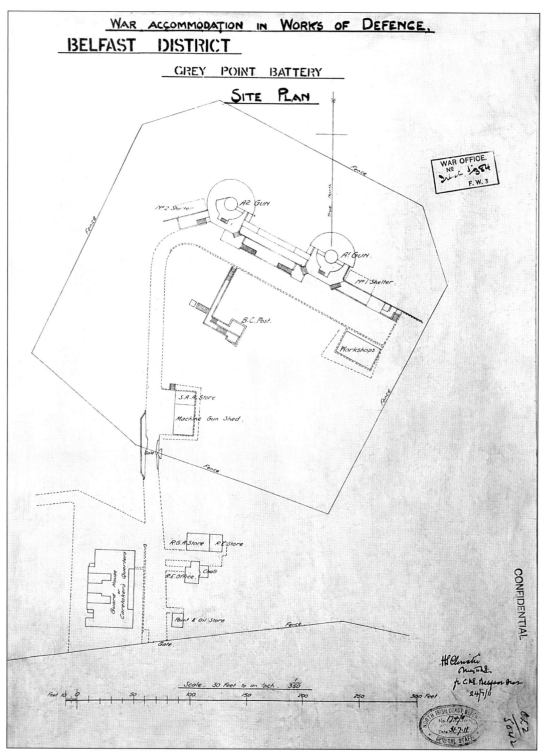

Plan of Grey Point Fort, 1911.

PRO WO 78/4784

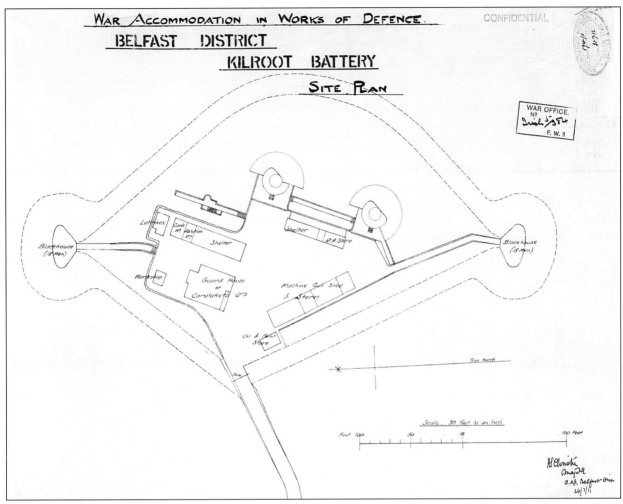

WAR ACCOMMODATION IN WORKS OF DEFENCE.

BELFAST DISTRICT

KILROOT BATTERY

SITE PLAN

CONFIDENTIAL

WAR OFFICE.
No
F. W. 3

Blockhouse
(18 men)

Latrines

Cook
Ho Ablution
Rm

Shelter

Shelter

R.A. Store

Blockhouse
(18 men)

Workshop

Guard House
or
Caretakers Qrs

Machine Gun Shed
& Stores

Oil & Paint
Store

True North

Scale. 30 Feet to an Inch

Feet 100   50   0   100 Feet

Plan of Kilroot Fort, 1911.

PRO WO 78/4748

At the same time the 6-inch (152-mm) BL Mk VI guns at Dunree were replaced with the two new Mk VIIs. This involved modifying the gun positions and the work was carried out by the contractor, Messrs Campbell and Sons of Belfast, a firm now much experienced in fortification work. The guns were in place by 1912 and hutted accommodation for a further 96 men was also provided, together with an improved water supply system for the whole fort.

No mention was made of the Belfast forts in the defence schemes of 1906 as the new forts were not completed until 1907 and 1910 and Belfast was the last commercial port in the United Kingdom to be fortified in peacetime. Grey Point Fort was the first to be completed in 1907, followed by Kilroot in 1910. Each fort comprised two concrete gun positions for the barbette

mountings of the guns with a magazine, shell store and shelter built underneath. Grey Point Fort was pentagonal in shape and faced north-east towards the lough entrance. It was surrounded by a wall on top of which was an 'unclimbable' palisade. The battery command post was sited on a slight rise behind the guns. Immediately inside the main entrance to the fort was a store for the movable armament of three .303-inch (7.6-mm) Maxim machine-guns on field carriages.

At Kilroot Fort the layout of the gun positions, which faced east, the magazine, shell store and shelter were identical to that of Grey Point. The overall shape of the fort differed in being roughly diamond-shaped rather than pentagonal but like Grey Point Fort it too was surrounded by a wall. The fort was defended by two large blockhouses projecting into the ditch at the northern and southern ends of the diamond. These blockhouses were each capable of holding 18 men and were cam-shaped, with the narrow rear angle adjoining the interior of the fort and permitting entrance by means of a narrow covered way. The shape of the blockhouses enabled the defenders to bring down rifle fire along the complete length of the ditch. Kilroot Fort was also provided with a movable armament of three Maxim .303-inch (7.6-mm) machine guns.

Like the Lough Swilly forts, the garrisons for Grey Point and Kilroot were found from 15th Company RGA and one company of the Antrim Royal Garrison Artillery (Special Reserve), the new title of the old Antrim Artillery Militia. This unit had changed its title in 1907 when all the Irish militia artillery units, with the exception of the Cork and Antrim Artillery Militias, had been disbanded on the formation of the new Territorial Force. These two units were tasked with manning the Irish coast defences and, as no Territorial Force units were raised in Ireland, became units of the Special Reserve. The Antrim Artillery continued to train at Carrickfergus Castle where, in 1902, the practice battery was modernised. In the Garden Battery, alongside the castle, two of the mountings for 64-pdr RML guns were removed and replaced by two 5-inch (127-mm) BL guns.[6] In addition, the Antrim Royal Garrison Artillery (Special Reserve) provided two companies to man the Belfast movable armament of eight old 15-pdr BLC Mk IV field guns which were to provide support for the infantry battalions designated to protect Belfast from attack by an enemy landing force.

The defence schemes were revised on a regular basis and the Belfast scheme was next reviewed in 1912. Then there were only minor changes involving re-allocation of the militia and infantry battalions and the establishing of the Port War Signal Station at Orlock Point near Groomsport. There was, however, a change in the movable armament for the defence of the Belfast forts. The military authorities were worried about the

possibility of a night raid on the Belfast docks by boats carrying small parties of saboteurs armed with explosives. There were two main navigation channels into the docks, the Victoria Channel and the Musgrave Channel, and between these two channels there was a spit of land called East Twin Island. Opposite it on the other side of the Victoria Channel was its twin, West Twin Island. The War Office leased the end of East Twin Island and established a small hutted camp for a garrison of 50 men. Along the water's edge, facing up the two channels, a wall and a protective embankment was built with emplacements for two .303-inch (7.6-mm) Maxim machine-guns. These guns were provided by reducing the number of machine-guns allocated to Grey Point and Kilroot forts by one each.

The two Belfast forts were not only built to designs incorporating modern principles of fortification but their design also took into consideration the political situation in the country at that time. Attack from the land fronts by disaffected local people was now more than just a remote possibility as a result of the unrest generated by the latest proposals for Irish Home Rule and the resulting disturbed state of Ulster. The Ulster Volunteer Force, now 90,000 strong, was arming to fight against any attempt to force Home Rule on the province and it was by no means certain that civil war could be avoided. The British military authorities considered it prudent, therefore, to ensure that all the coastal forts in Ulster were made self-defensible in order to reduce, as far as possible, their vulnerability to a coup de main. Unlike Kilroot Fort, neither Lenan nor Dunree in Lough Swilly, or Grey Point had been provided with blockhouses for defence from attack from the landward side. So in 1913 the defences of these forts were reviewed and plans were drawn up for the construction of a number of concrete blockhouses to protect the land fronts of the forts. Despite this review, however, no work on building the blockhouses had been started before the outbreak of war on 4 August 1914.

10 World War One 1914–1918

The outbreak of war

The first six months of 1914 were an eventful time in Ulster. The British government was determined to force through Home Rule for the whole of Ireland and the unionists in the province were just as determined to oppose it, by armed force if necessary. Sir Edward Carson had raised the Ulster Volunteer Force (UVF), almost 90,000 strong, and on the night of 24/25 April 1914 30,000 modern rifles were smuggled into Ulster through the small ports of Larne, Bangor and Donaghadee to arm the UVF. Ulster was poised on the brink of armed rebellion and it was only the assassination in far-off Serbia of the Archduke Ferdinand, heir to the throne of Austria-Hungary, in July 1914 that brought the Ulster Protestants back from the brink.

On 29 July the forces of the Crown in Ireland received orders to implement what was termed the 'Precautionary Stage' in the defence schemes. This was the immediate stage before war and involved the manning of certain fixed defences to ensure that an enemy could not carry out a successful surprise attack, together with the preparation of field works and obstructions. At Belfast, which was not considered vulnerable to a surprise attack, the fixed defences were not manned at this stage and precautions were limited to placing guards on the dock gates. In Londonderry the 15th Company RGA was alerted and part of the company, together with personnel of 33rd Fortress Company RE, moved to its war location to man the Lough Swilly forts. The rationale here was that as Lough Swilly was a potential naval base it might be vulnerable to an attack by enemy minelayers.

At Orlock Point, between Bangor and Groomsport, at the entrance to Belfast Lough and at Fanad Head at the entrance to Lough Swilly the Port War Signal Stations were manned. The function of these stations was the identification of warships approaching the port or harbour and the passage of this information by telephone to the naval headquarters and the Army fortress commander. The Precautionary Stage was quickly followed by the second, or 'Emergency', stage which involved the mobilisation of naval and military reserves. The Antrim Royal Garrison Artillery (Special Reserve) mobilised at their headquarters at Carrickfergus Castle and one company was dispatched to man Kilroot Fort, now the examination battery for Belfast Lough. A second company was moved to Grey Point to assist 15th Company RGA in manning that fort and two more companies were sent to Lough Swilly to assist in the manning of Lenan and Dunree forts. Reserve infantry battalions were mobilised and these provided the troops to protect the forts and other vulnerable points. The three battalions allocated for the defence of Lough Swilly were the 3rd and 4th Bns The Royal Inniskilling Fusiliers (SR) and the 3rd Bn The Royal Irish Fusiliers (SR). At Belfast the battalions were the 3rd, 4th and 5th Bns The Royal Irish Rifles (SR).[1] Finally, on 4 August 1914 Great Britain declared war on Germany.

With Britain now in a state of war with Germany, naval control measures were initiated at all the defended ports throughout the country. The Examination Service was established at each port with the role of controlling the entry into the port of all merchant shipping and other vessels other than naval vessels. At each port an area of water was designated as the examination anchorage where all non-naval vessels entering the port had to anchor and await inspection if required to do so by the examination officer. This anchorage was covered by the guns of the examination battery, the role of which was, when necessary, to force any ship to stop by firing a shell across its bow or even sinking it if it refused to stop. This battery was always manned throughout daylight hours. At Lough Swilly the examination battery was the battery in Dunree Fort.

The main base for the Grand Fleet, as the British main battle fleet was now named, was Scapa Flow in the Orkneys. However, in the first three months of war, Scapa remained completely unprotected thanks to pre-war

Royal Navy battleships and heavy cruisers pictured in Lough Swilly circa 1911. The warship lying to the left beyond the yacht is the battleship HMS *King Edward VII*. *National Library of Ireland*

parsimoniousness on the part of HM Treasury. This was despite the fact that Scapa was the only base and anchorage on the east coast large enough to accommodate all the Grand Fleet at one time. On 1 September 1914 a submarine was reported in Scapa Flow as the Grand Fleet lay at anchor. Although this was probably a false alarm, despite numerous ships reporting sightings, the effect was somewhat similar to that of a fox in a hen house. It was clear that the Grand Fleet base must be made secure against submarine attack and until it was the only answer was for the Grand Fleet to remain at sea as much as possible. Between the beginning of September and the end of December 1914 the Grand Fleet was at sea for virtually the whole time, with only six days spent at Loch Ewe on the west coast of Scotland in September and two weeks in Lough Swilly in October for gunnery practice.

Lough Swilly provided a convenient temporary base for the fleet because it was a defended port and, as such, possessed an organisation which regulated the entry of ships. On 17 October the 3rd and 6th Battle Squadrons, the 2nd Cruiser Squadron and the 1st Light Cruiser Squadron arrived in the lough to be followed five days later by the 1st and 4th Battle Squadrons with two divisions of destroyers. The water of the lough was so shallow as to make it difficult for a submarine to enter submerged, but, nevertheless, steps were taken immediately to lay an anti-submarine obstruction at the entrance to the lough. Wire hawsers were suspended at varying depths between six colliers which were anchored across the entrance to the lough, with target rafts as intermediate supports and the whole area was patrolled by armed steamers and drifters with destroyers in support. In due course this temporary obstruction was replaced by a boom and anti-submarine net laid between Macamish Point on the western shore and Ned's Point on

HMS *Audacious* sinking at the entrance to Lough Swilly on 27th October 1914.   *Imperial War Museum*

the eastern side. Despite these precautions disaster struck on 27 October when the new battleship HMS *Audacious* hit a mine laid by the German auxiliary cruiser SMS *Berlin* at the entrance to Lough Swilly and subsequently sank with considerable loss of life.

However, the Grand Fleet could not threaten the German High Seas Fleet from a base in Lough Swilly, useful as the lough was for gunnery training. So on 3 November the Grand Fleet left the lough and for the remainder of that month and during December it continued mostly at sea, but in a position to blockade the entrance to the North Sea and strike at the German fleet should it leave its own bases. Lough Swilly returned to its normal routine existence.

Lough Swilly

In the months following the outbreak of war the War Office decided to implement the earlier plan to improve the land defences of the forts at Lenan and Dunree by the construction of a number of blockhouses. Originally planned in 1913, work did not start on these new defences until early in 1916 when a line of eight concrete

Blockhouse on the redoubt at Fort Dunree.   *Author*

Lenan Head Fort showing one of the blockhouses built to defend the ditch with a loopholed wall behind.   *Author*

The Admiralty pier at Rathmullen with the oil storage tank built on the terreplein of the old fort.   *Author's collection*

blockhouses loopholed for rifles was built at Dunree. The line ran from the small bay immediately north of the redoubt to a cove on the southern shore of the headland with three blockhouses north of the redoubt, three to the south and two built on top of the redoubt itself.

Two sections of rubble stone wall 4 feet 6 inches (1.38 metres) high, each aligned in a shallow V-shape, were built, one between the redoubt wall and the next blockhouse to the south and the second between that blockhouse and the entrance to the camp adjoining the fort. In front of the blockhouses there was a line of barbed wire entanglement. The majority of the blockhouses were either hexagonal or octagonal in shape with iron shutters protecting the loopholes.[2] Protection was also provided for the men manning the two 6-inch (152-mm) guns against sniper fire by installing a loop-holed wall behind each gun position. This concrete wall was about seven feet (2.15 metres) high with an overhead projection which acted as a narrow roof. Each wall was sited to cover the right rear section of each gun position.

At Lenan the problem of the land front defence was made easier by the existing ditch which protected that side of the fort. The two gun positions were protected from observation and enemy fire by a rise in the ground to the rear of the positions but the accommodation buildings, stores and workshops were completely open to fire from the south and east. The solution, as far as the engineer staff of Belfast District were concerned, was to build three blockhouses or caponiers to defend the ditch and two loopholed walls backed by shallow trenches. In addition, a concrete fire trench was built into the higher ground near the cliff edge overlooking the north-eastern section of the ditch.

Two of the blockhouses were diamond-shaped and one

One of the 6-inch (152-mm) BL Mk VII guns of Dunree Battery.
Author

was pentagonal. All three had rifle loopholes which, like those at Dunree, were protected by iron shutters. Approach to each blockhouse was along a short covered-way leading down steps into the blockhouse. A raised earth bank provided some cover from both fire and view for the approach to the pentagonal blockhouse at the north-eastern end of the ditch, but the approach to the other two blockhouses was over open ground. To overcome this problem the engineers built an underground shelter close to each covered way. The shelters were each protected by means of an earth bank and a low rubble-stone wall three feet (0.9 metres) high. The latter had a shallow trench 18 inches (45 cm) deep immediately behind it. Each wall had two narrow stone traverses and the entrance to each shelter was also protected by a traverse, made of earth, seven feet (2.15 metres) high.[3] These were the only improvements made to the defences of Lough Swilly during the war except for the construction of a position finding cell on Dunaff Head in 1918.

In 1914 and early 1915 the 3rd Bn The Royal Irish

Fusiliers (SR) was stationed in and around Dunree Fort while the two battalions of The Royal Inniskilling Fusiliers allocated for the defence of the Innishowen Fortress were accommodated in Ludden Camp at Buncrana and Glenfield Camp at Clonmany. Throughout the war, infantry battalions in training were stationed around Lough Swilly but as the conflict continued the main role of the lough became that of a naval base. The German submarine campaign against Allied merchant shipping meant that by mid-1917 the lough had become a major base for destroyers and sloops escorting merchant ships sailing in the newly established convoy system.

Buncrana became the headquarters of one of 23 naval patrol areas that were established in home waters. A rear admiral was in command and in July 1917 16 destroyers and 11 sloops were based in Lough Swilly. Within three months this force had been increased to 30 destroyers, 13 sloops, 13 submarines in two flotillas, and a seaplane carrier, thus reflecting the rapidly increasing importance of the lough as an anti-submarine base.[4] By April 1918 the submarines and the seaplane carrier had departed but the number of destroyers had increased to 38 in the 2nd and 3rd Destroyer Flotillas and the North Channel Patrol and the sloop flotilla had been reinforced by the five ships of the North Sea Hydrophone Flotilla.[5]

The old fort at Rathmullen was taken over by the Royal Navy in August 1917 and an oil fuel tank was built on the battery terreplein together with a pipeline and a new pier immediately in front of the fort. For a short period the fort was also used as the headquarters of a kite balloon section of the Royal Naval Air Service but was abandoned before the end of the war. Aerial activity had arrived in the lough firstly with the seaplane carrier in late 1917 and then, the following year, with the arrival of a kite balloon section of the Royal Naval Air Service. The kite balloons were observation balloons which were secured to Royal Navy vessels and merchant ships and their role was reconnaissance and observation. The use of kite balloons increased the range of observation available to a convoy and its escorts. The observer in the balloon was able to provide early warning of submarine attacks by locating U-Boats on the surface before they submerged in the final stages of their attack, and they could control naval gunfire when the escorting warships engaged the submarine.

Throughout most of the war Lough Foyle remained something of a military backwater. It was only in 1917 when the United States entered the war that a United States seaplane base was established on the shores of the lough, close to Londonderry.

Belfast Lough

The strategic importance of Belfast Lough was not due just to the 2.5 million tons of merchant shipping that used the port annually. It was also due to its shipyards and ship repair facilities and, in particular, the new Thomson Graving Dock which was large enough to take the latest Dreadnought battleships. Despite its importance in the early months of the war, Belfast was not considered to be under any immediate threat of attack and so no steps were taken to improve its defences. The guns of Grey Point Fort and Kilroot Fort could only be fought by day as no defence electric lights (searchlights) were provided for either fort. This can only be considered surprising in view of the fears of possible attacks by vessels carrying small parties of saboteurs whose target might well have been the new graving dock.

It was this threat of saboteurs together with the possibility of a submarine attacking the docks with gunfire which appears to have led to the installation of two 12-pdr QF guns at a new position on East Twin Island, one of the two spits of land flanking the entrance to the Victoria Channel which led into the docks.

Both these pieces of land were low-lying so it was decided that the guns of the new battery should be raised by placing them on square concrete towers 20 feet (6.15 metres) high and 14 feet (4.3 metres) wide. The towers were connected by a steel walkway on which, mid-way along, was the gun control post. In each of the towers, below the gun mounting, there was a shelter for the gun crew, and at the base of the right-hand tower and immediately in front of it was the director's post for the defence electric lights. At last the decision had been taken to install searchlights to enable the 12-pdr QF guns to be fought by night when the threat to the docks would probably be greatest. One 24-inch (61-cm) searchlight was installed to the right of the old pre-war machine gun positions and a second light was sited across the channel on West Twin Island. To defend the new gun position two circular concrete machine-gun emplacements were also

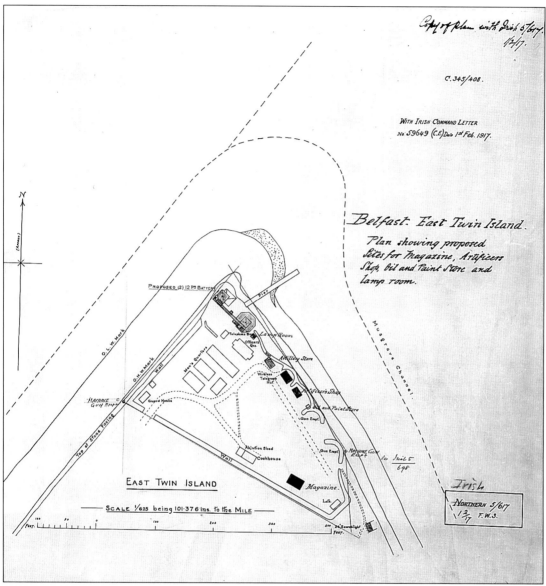

Plan of East Twin Island Battery, Belfast, 1917.

PRO WO 78/4872

built, one at the main entrance to the position covering the landward side and the other on the water's edge in front of the old musketry wall.[6]

At Grey Point three diamond-shaped blockhouses similar to those at Lenan fort were constructed to improve the land-front defence of the fort. One blockhouse was built at the centre of the northern wall with the other two at the fort's east and west corners. The fort was completely surrounded by a wide barbed wire entanglement and the blockhouses acted as caponiers enabling rifle fire to be directed against an enemy

attempting to break through the wire. Kilroot Fort was similarly surrounded by barbed wire.

During World War One, Belfast was used primarily as a trawler base by the Royal Navy. Immediately after the outbreak of war it became apparent that German submarine activity in the Irish Sea must be prevented or, at least, reduced to the very minimum. St George's Channel at the southern end of the Irish Sea was too wide to be controlled in any other way than by patrolling but the North Channel was a different matter altogether. Here the distance between the Ulster coast and Scotland was only 16 miles (25 km) and so the Admiralty decided to close the gap using anti-submarine nets. Closing the North Channel was more easily planned than executed. In places the depth of the channel was 420 feet (129 metres) and it was not possible to lay a single net to that depth. To the Admiralty experts the answer lay in forcing the submarines to the surface by laying nets in sequence over a considerable distance so that it wasn't just a matter of negotiating only one net. By 1918 the North Channel anti-submarine nets covered an area in the shape of a parallelogram 20 miles (32 km) long by 12 miles (19.2 km) wide between Rathlin Island and the Mull of Kintyre.

A passage was left for merchant shipping between Rathlin Island and the mainland and so down the Antrim coast. The total of 36 miles (57.6 km) of nets was maintained by 72 drifters, each drifter supporting half a mile (800 metres) of net. In total 130 drifters were detailed to support and patrol the nets, with three armed trawler units based on Belfast and Larne patrolling the southern end and the Belfast armed yacht squadron responsible for the northern end.[7]

In addition to the armed trawlers, airships of the Royal Naval Air Service were used to patrol the North Channel and an airship mooring station was established at Bentra, about half a mile (800 metres) north-west of Whitehead, on the northern shore of the lough. It was a sub-station of the larger airship station at Luce Bay across the North

Channel near Stranraer and was commissioned early in 1917. It was equipped with a single, large, canvas covered portable airship shed which measured 150 feet long, 45 feet wide and 50 feet high (46x13.8x15.3 metres) and was designed to house SS-type non-rigid dirigibles.

As the war drew to a close, a number of changes occurred in the organisation of the North Irish coast defences. In August 1918 the examination battery at Dunree Fort was handed over to the Royal Navy and in the following month the RGA defence at home was reorganised into Fire Commands. Those elements of the Antrim Royal Garrison Artillery (Special Reserve) and the 15th Company RGA manning the defences of Belfast Lough were absorbed into the new No 34 (Antrim) Fire Command with its headquarters at Carrickfergus. The remaining personnel of these units, those manning the Lough Swilly defences, became No 35 (Donegal) Fire Command with headquarters at Lenan Fort.[8]

None of the North Irish forts and batteries fired a shot in anger during the whole of the war, yet they were an essential element of the defences of the United Kingdom throughout those four long years. In effect the guns and gunners of the coast defence forts provided a successful deterrent against attacks by both German surface warships and submarines on the two loughs which provided bases so vital to success in the naval war.

Between the Wars 1919–1939

The Troubles

The immediate result of the cessation of hostilities between Germany and the Allies in November 1918 and the peace conference the following year was that by 1920 all coast batteries at defended ports in the United Kingdom were reduced to a care and maintenance status. Only the Irish forts retained any form of a garrison because of the unsettled political situation in the country.

Ever since the Easter Rebellion in 1916 militant Irish nationalist feelings had been growing stronger, the flames of nationalism fuelled by the inept handling of the aftermath of the rebellion by the British government. The execution of the leaders of the rebellion on the orders of the British government increased recruiting for Sinn Féin and the secretive Irish Republican Brotherhood, as did the abortive attempt to impose conscription in 1918. As a result by 1919 Sinn Féin had declared a republic and set up a parallel administration to the British authority in Ireland with its own parliament (Dáil Éireann), national bank, courts of justice and police force.

The Irish nationalists expected Great Britain to implement the Home Rule Act of 1914 as soon as the war ended but by then the situation had changed considerably. In negotiations between Redmond for the Irish nationalists and Carson for the Ulster unionists, Lloyd George, the British Prime Minister, persuaded both men to recommend to their supporters a plan for Home Rule which excluded six of the Ulster counties (Antrim, Armagh, Down, Fermanagh, Tyrone and Londonderry). The remaining three counties, Donegal, Cavan and Monaghan, were to be included with the 26 Home Rule counties. The nationalists accepted this plan with reluctance, believing the exclusion of the six counties to be only a temporary measure. Once it was clear that Redmond had been tricked by Lloyd George, Sinn Féin commenced a guerrilla war against the British administration which was to increase in ferocity until a truce was negotiated in 1921.

During this period, usually known as 'The Troubles', the British troops at Dunree and Lenan were little affected by the activities of the IRA though the wisdom of improving the land front defences of the two forts quickly became apparent. Unlike Bere Island in Bantry Bay and Spike Island in Cork Harbour, Dunree was not considered suitable for use as an internment camp for nationalist prisoners and this fact may have helped to maintain the good relations that existed between the British garrison and the local civilians which lasted for the next 18 years.

The truce in July 1921 led on in October to negotiations for a treaty. The IRA had made Ireland ungovernable but they had not succeeded in driving the British out. On the other hand the British people were tired of war and had little stomach for the draconian measures that would be necessary to crush the nationalists who now had the sympathy of most of the Irish population. The result was the usual political compromise. The Irish did not get the republic they desired: instead Michael Collins, who led the nationalist delegation in London, accepted a form of dominion status for the 26 counties, now to be known as the Irish Free State or, in gaelic, Éire.

Under Article 6 of the Treaty, responsibility for the defence by sea of Great Britain and Ireland was to be undertaken by His Majesty's Imperial Forces, though this situation was to be reviewed at an Anglo-Irish conference after five years. Article 7 guaranteed His Majesty's Imperial Forces the use of certain harbours and facilities in time of peace as laid down in the annex to the Treaty and, in time of war, such harbours and other facilities as the British government should require. The specific facilities as indicated in the annex included the harbour defences of Queenstown (Cork), Berehaven in Bantry Bay and Lough Swilly.

The signing of the Treaty did not bring to an end the guerrilla war that had plagued Ireland for over almost three years. Certainly hostilities between the British forces in the new Irish Free State and the IRA ceased and in 1922 the British began to withdraw their forces. However, civil war now broke out between the forces of the new state and dissident members of the IRA who refused to accept the terms of the Treaty and, in particular, the new form of dominion status within the British Empire instead of a republic outside it.

This civil war between the so-called republicans and the Irish Free State government was extremely bitter. The republicans could not accept the exclusion of the six Ulster counties and so operations were carried out within the boundaries of the British-controlled Northern Ireland. Understandably the new government at Stormont saw both the legitimate forces of the Irish Free State and the dissident republicans as a threat to the stability of Northern Ireland. Indeed, the republicans carried out raids against RIC barracks inside Northern Ireland, burnt railway stations and attacked members of the RIC and the newly-formed Ulster Special Constabulary, while, in retaliation Protestant mobs attacked Catholics in Londonderry and Belfast and burnt their property. Operations against the republicans were carried out by the RIC and members of the 'A' and 'B' Special Constabulary, but British troops remained in Northern Ireland as a garrison.

In May 1922 dissident Republicans expelled local Unionist civilians from the small Donegal border village of Pettigo and occupied the village of Belleek, part of which was now in Northern Ireland. The old fort at Belleek, on the Donegal side of the border, became a base from which raids were launched into west Fermanagh. The unionists in the Pettigo–Belleek triangle requested help from the Northern Ireland government and a force of 50 'A' and 'B' Specials was dispatched to Belleek. The force had to travel by boat across Lough Erne as the only road into the village from Northern Ireland actually passed through a small portion of the Irish Free State. The detachment of special constables was attacked by a strong force of republicans, was besieged in Magherameenagh Castle and a relief force was fired on from Belleek fort. The republicans continued to reinforce Belleek and Pettigo without hindrance from the Free State Army, so the decision was taken by the county commandant of the Ulster Special Constabulary to evacuate the triangle.

Although the seizure of the triangle caused a considerable stir in London, the British government was unwilling to take any immediate action for fear of upsetting the delicate negotiations which were then in progress with the Free State government concerning the constitution of the new state. The Free State government blamed the occupation of the triangle on IRA 'irregulars' and by doing so appeared to give their blessing to British action to expel the republicans occupying Northern Ireland territory.

The British Army was ordered to carry out the operation to reoccupy Belleek and disperse the republican forces in the triangle. The formation responsible for this task was the 17th Infantry Brigade with three infantry battalions, a howitzer battery and some armoured cars. Pettigo, despite being within the Irish Free State, was occupied by elements of the brigade on 4 June, and on the following day a British force advanced on Belleek in two columns, one along the northern shore of Lough Erne and the other along the southern shore. The advance guard of the southern column came under heavy fire from Belleek fort in Donegal. Fire was returned and the howitzer battery fired about 20 rounds of high explosive shell, four of which were directed at the fort without, apparently, doing very much damage to the structure. The republican garrison quickly retreated and the fort was occupied without further opposition and remained in British hands for over two years until 24 August 1924.

Built to help the British defend Belleek against civil unrest, to protect the bridge and guard the approach to Enniskillen, it was ironical that when the fort was assaulted for the only time in its history the attackers were units of the British Army.

Two other fortifications in Ulster were caught up in the 'Troubles' of the 1920s. As the Free State forces gradually eliminated republican opposition in the Inishowen Peninsula, some of the remaining republicans occupied the disarmed fort on Inch. About 100 republicans occupied the fort and some crossed over to Rathmelton to establish another base in the town. The republicans held the fort for over a week and it was clear that the Free State troops would need more than small arms to capture it. During the week that they held the fort the republicans exchanged fire with the Free State troops across the water at Fahan. They attempted to stop the use of the railway to Buncrana by sniping at the trains as they passed Inch. This brought about an almost laughable situation where the Lough Swilly trains continued to run each day: the Free State troops held their fire as the trains passed their positions and the railway company counselled the passengers to lie on the floor of the carriages as the trains passed through Fahan. On the 14 July 1922, the *Londonderry Sentinel* reported:

A gunboat flying the Irish flag and under the control, it is understood, of the Free State authorities, arrived in Lough Swilly . . . and during the day quantities of war material were landed at Buncrana. Interesting developments are expected.

The war material included armoured cars and one 18-pdr QF field gun which was positioned at Fahan and opened fire on the fort at 19.00 hours on Saturday, 15 July. This was a clear indication that the Free State forces meant business and on the following day the fort was assaulted. After a token resistance, Captain Mullen, who had earlier in the month described himself in a letter to the *Londonderry Sentinel* as the "executive officer commanding Inch Fort", surrendered with 20 of his men. This was the the only occasion any of the forts of Lough Swilly came under any form of attack.

In Northern Ireland itself, on Friday, 18 August 1922, republicans opened fire with small arms on B Specials garrisoning the Martello tower at Magilligan Point. Shots were fired at the tower from a position near Greencastle across the River Foyle in Donegal. The B Specials were using the tower as a base and observation post (OP) to prevent republicans crossing into Northern Ireland at the narrowest part of the lough. A number of local people were enjoying the pleasant summer evening and were forced unceremoniously to take cover but no one was injured. Fire was not returned and the republicans made no further attempt to engage the B Specials' position.

Treaty Port

The civil war in the Irish Free State ended in April 1923 and the forts of Lough Swilly settled down to the uneventful routine of peacetime. The four defended ports in Ireland – Cork, Berehaven, Lough Swilly and Belfast – continued to be garrisoned by regular troops even after the review of coast defences carried out by the War Office in 1926. This review resulted in the responsibility for manning the coast batteries in Britain passing to units of the Territorial Army (TA). In Ireland there were no TA units and the two Special Reserve regiments – the Cork RGA (SR) and the Antrim RGA (SR) – had been disbanded at the end of the war. So the three defended ports now in the Irish Free State were manned by five heavy batteries of the Royal Artillery and the garrisons of the Belfast forts were provided by elements of the battery which also provided the garrisons for the Lough Swilly forts.

For administrative matters the forts were placed under the command of the GOC Northern Ireland District but for all other purposes they came under the command of the GOC-in-C Western Command in England. The garrison of the two forts was provided by 17th Heavy Battery RA and in 1932 the strength was ten officers and 157 other ranks. Communication between Dunree and Lenan was by means of a twenty-line submarine cable, while for communication with Londonderry and Belfast, wireless was used. The garrison included a Royal Signals detachment of a sergeant, a corporal and four signallers with four wireless stations Type 'C', two for each fort.

Although money was tight, some improvements to Dunree Camp were made. In 1930 additional quarters were built together with a squash court. In 1933 improvements were made to the electric power generation system and more modern engines installed to power the searchlights. The positions of the searchlights had been changed and one of the lights had been moved into the old fort and the other to the area of the practice battery. The old searchlight positions were converted into the paint store and the carpenter's shop.

Some years earlier, in 1924, the Admiralty wanted the guns at Lenan Fort to be converted to long-range mountings which permitted an angle of fire of 35 degrees rather than an angle of 15 degrees with the existing mountings. The justification for the proposed change was that a convoy anchorage in Lough Swilly was open to bombardment by enemy raiders from Sheephaven to the west. Although it was recommended by the Joint Overseas and Home Defence Committee, a sub-committee of the Committee of Imperial Defence, this change to long-range mountings was never made. Nor was any form of anti-aircraft defence provided for Lough Swilly because of what was considered to be the remoteness of the chances of attack by seaborne aircraft. The committee considered that the anti-aircraft defence of any convoy while at anchor in the lough would be provided by the guns of the escort vessels and this would be sufficient.[1] The following year the two 4.7-inch (120-mm) QF guns mounted on the old fort at Dunree were removed, as had been recommended by the Owen Committee almost 20 years earlier, and replaced by two 12-pdr QF guns. In addition, two 18-pdr QF field guns were provided for each fort as a mobile armament for use against hostile landings or against 'local marauding bands', meaning, of course, the IRA. The final change in armament came in 1936 when the mobile armament for each fort was changed to two 4.5-inch (115-mm) howitzers and two Vickers .303-inch (7.6-mm) machine guns.

While the garrisons of Dunree and Lenan maintained good relations with the local inhabitants of the Inishowen Peninsula, a fact confirmed by the number of local girls marrying soldiers of the garrison, the existence of the Treaty ports as such continued to bedevil relations between Great Britain and the Irish Free State. To fervent nationalists the continued existence of British troops on Free State soil meant that the independence gained as a result of the Treaty was, in fact, a sham. To serious military thinkers a more practical problem resulted from the existence of the Treaty ports. Clause 7 of the Treaty permitted Great Britain in time of war or strained relations with a foreign power to make use of such harbours and other facilities in Ireland as were considered necessary for the defence of Great Britain. Because of British control of Irish ports and other facilities, the Irish Free State would find it almost impossible to proclaim its neutrality in any future conflict involving Great Britain.

In 1932 the general election in the Irish Free State was won by the Fianna Fáil party and its leader, Eamon de Valera, became President of the Executive Council. In his first six years of office it was de Valera's main aim to bring about the dismemberment of the Treaty that he had so steadfastly opposed since it had been signed in 1922. His first act was to ask the King to withdraw the governor general and this was followed by the removal of the oath of allegiance. In addition, he directed that the land annuities – interest payments on loans which the British government had advanced to Irish tenant farmers at the end of the previous century to enable them to purchase their land – should no longer be paid. This resulted in an economic war when the British government placed a 20% duty on all Irish goods entering Britain and the Free State government retaliated with tariffs on British goods entering the Free State.

The main effect of this trade war was to cause considerable hardship to the owners of the larger farms in Ireland who found their British markets closed to them

British troops manning the fort at Belleek, 1922.

Belfast Central Library

and so, by 1935, tentative steps were taken by the Irish to end this unhappy state of affairs. In 1936 a number of secret meetings were held between de Valera and Malcolm MacDonald, the Dominions Secretary in Baldwin's government, with a view to discussing the trade war, constitutional issues and defence. However, it was made clear to de Valera by MacDonald that the matter of partition was was not up for discussion.

While the secret talks were being held with the representatives of the British government, de Valera was working on a new constitution to replace the one created by the Treaty. The Constitution of Éire (Ireland) abolished the oath of allegiance to the king and claimed sovereignty over all 32 counties of Ireland. Although the king was still recognised as head of the Commonwealth, the position of the king's representative in Ireland was abolished and the new post of President of Éire introduced. The British government, although unhappy, accepted the changes reluctantly but with as much grace as it could muster since, in effect, there was little it could do about them.

Eamon de Valera then proceeded to raise the matter of the Treaty ports with the British Prime Minister, Neville Chamberlain, Baldwin's successor. Chamberlain was anxious to normalise political relations with the Irish, and

A 12-pdr QF gun mounted in the old fort at Dunree.   *Author*

the British military authorities had doubts about the wisdom of retaining the ports. While there was no doubt about the strategic importance of the ports, the British generals were worried about the size of forces needed to defend the ports against a hostile Irish population. To add to these doubts the Committee of Imperial Defence in early 1938 estimated that it would cost about £650,000 to modernise the defences of the three Treaty ports, including providing additional equipment such as booms and indicator loops. For Lough Swilly this included the modernisation of the two 9.2-inch (233-mm) BL guns at Lenan Fort and the construction of a new port war signal station on Dunaff Head to replace the old station which had been burnt down.[2]

Although Winston Churchill and other Conservative backbench MPs were bitterly opposed to any amendment to sections 6 and 7 of the Treaty, particularly in view of the worsening political situation in Europe, Chamberlain pressed ahead with negotiations for a new Anglo-Irish agreement which was signed on 25 April 1938. Under this agreement the provisions of the 1921 Treaty covering

the reserved ports were abolished and in return the Irish government gave an assurance that the ports would not be used against the British in any future war.[3]

Six months later, in October 1938, both Dunree and Lenan forts together with their armament were handed over to the Irish Free State Army. The handover of the armament of the Treaty ports had been the subject of detailed negotiation as to which guns and what equipment constituted part of the 'fixed defences' and which were for training purposes and local defence, the latter equipment being retained by the British Army. In the end the British authorities handed over the four heavy guns at Lough Swilly while the Irish Army purchased the four 4.5-inch (114-mm) QF howitzers provided for local defence but declined to purchase the four Vickers medium machine-guns. The handover, on a wet and windy autumn day, was a very low-key affair with only a handful of troops from each army present. On the day of the handover the Irish Army created two new artillery units to garrison the Lough Swilly forts. The garrison for Dunree was provided by 5th Coast Battery, Artillery Corps while 6th Coast Battery was formed at Lenan Fort. Both these units were composed of elements from the permanent and the reserve forces.

At Lenan Fort, Lieutenant Callaghan of the Irish Army took over from Major Mersey Thompson MC, RA and at Fort Dunree Lieutenant Donagh took over from Major GE Laing MM, RA. The Union flag was lowered and the Irish tricolour was raised in its place, and the fact that the British sergeant lowering the Union flag and the Irish sergeant raising the tricolour at Dunree were brothers-in-law was, perhaps, evidence of the good relations existing at that time between the British garrisons and the local people. The British troops then boarded troop-carrying lorries and were driven across the border to Londonderry railway station.

Northern Ireland

With the end of the civil war in the Irish Free State in 1923, republican operations against Northern Ireland decreased but did not cease altogether. However, without effective external support the IRA within the province also found it more and more difficult to oppose effectively the newly formed Royal Ulster Constabulary (RUC) and the Ulster Special Constabulary (USC). By October 1923 conditions in Belfast were reported to be peaceable and the War Office began to reduce the Army

garrison from 12 battalions to five battalions, a howitzer battery and an armoured car company. The defences of Belfast Lough, now virtually reduced to care and maintenance, were manned by elements of 17th Heavy Battery RA which also provided the Lough Swilly garrison.

Steps were also taken by the War Office to dispose of those forts and batteries considered surplus to requirements and the first to go was East Twin Island

British and Irish troops fraternising after the handover of Fort Dunree to the Irish army in October 1938.

Londonderry Sentinel, by permission of the British Library

Battery. Initially the Home Ports Defence Committee considered in 1920 that the battery should be retained but by November 1921 that decision had been reversed and instructions were issued that the battery should be dismantled and the site handed back to the Belfast Harbour Commissioners.[4] In 1928 Carrickfergus Castle was also relinquished and handed over to the Northern Ireland Ministry of Finance which became responsible for its maintenance as a scheduled ancient monument.

The problem facing the War Office in this period of intense financial stringency was how to find the most economic method of manning the Belfast defences. In Great Britain it had been possible to reduce the number of Regular Army heavy batteries manning the coast defences by using the Territorial Army but this was not possible in Northern Ireland as the Territorial Force Act did not apply there. Therefore, in its contingency planning the War Office allocated the Lancashire and Cheshire Heavy Brigade RA (TA) and the Renfrew Fortress Company RE (TA) to man Grey Point and Kilroot forts, and both these units attended annual camps

in Belfast for a number of years.

In the late 1920s the Home Ports Defence Committee had placed all the United Kingdom ports into one of three categories. These were: Category A – ports to which adequate defences should be installed in peacetime, to be fully manned before the outbreak of hostilities; Category B – ports to which adequate defences should be installed in peacetime to be manned as soon as possible after the outbreak of hostilities; and Category C – ports at which it would not be necessary to install defences in peacetime but for which defence schemes should be prepared to meet probable war requirements.

Belfast was classified as a Category B port where the defences should be manned as soon as possible after the outbreak of hostilities, but the garrison still had to mobilise in Great Britain and then move to Belfast. This problem was compounded by the fact that Belfast was one of the ports where the Examination Service was planned to be set up at the beginning of the precautionary period and this required the manning of at least one battery to act as the examination battery.

To the Home Ports Defence Committee the logical answer was to place Belfast on the same footing as the other defended ports in Great Britain and man the forts using a locally enlisted Territorial Army unit rather than a heavy battery of the Regular Army. Indeed in 1928 the committee complained that five heavy batteries were

Grey Point Fort, 1938.

Colonel I B Gailey

"locked up in Ireland".[5] The committee felt that there might be constitutional difficulties in raising a Territorial Army unit in Northern Ireland even though this was the cheapest option and the one favoured by the War Office. The Dominions Office believed that if coast defences in Northern Ireland became the responsibility of a locally raised corps, the Irish Free State government might suggest that their own units, similarly raised, might provide the personnel for manning the three defended ports in the Irish Free State.[6] The committee considered that raising a Supplementary Reserve unit in Northern Ireland might overcome the Dominions Office objection and might be a possible option.

The following year the committee considered the matter again. By this time the Northern Ireland government had been consulted and their reply was particularly interesting. The Northern Ireland government raised no objection to the application of the Territorial Force Act to Northern Ireland provided no local infantry units were formed.[7] Obviously the Unionist government feared that if such units were formed not all those receiving training in small arms and infantry tactics

Personnel of 188th Heavy Battery RA (TA) and the Antrim Fortress Company RE (TA) at their first annual camp at Grey Point Fort in July 1938.

Trustees of 74th (Antrim Artillery) Engineer Regiment RE (Volunteers)

would necessarily be unionist supporters!

Despite the decision to reconsider the whole matter at an early date, it was left in abeyance for almost ten years. This was mainly due to the tight control of public finance brought about by the economic depression in the years between 1929 and 1935. In 1936 the Committee of Imperial Defence again reviewed the problem of how to man the defences of Belfast. A memorandum from the Chief of the Imperial General Staff (CIGS) pointed out that the Admiralty had now re-classified Belfast as a Category A port requiring the defences to be manned before the outbreak of hostilities. However, under the current Belfast Defence Plan immediate manning of the defences could not be achieved as the personnel responsible for manning the defences – the Lancashire and Cheshire Heavy Brigade RA – had to travel from England to Belfast.

The CIGS suggested that as it was proposed to form an Auxiliary Air Force squadron in Northern Ireland – No 502 (Ulster) (Bomber) Squadron RAuxAF – it was now time to consider raising a heavy battery RA and a fortress company RE of the Territorial Army to man the Belfast defences. This time there was no objection from the Dominions Office which now felt that as the Irish Free State had formed a volunteer force of its own it would be difficult for that government to object to similar forces in Northern Ireland.[8] Once again the Stormont government indicated that it had no objection to the formation of Territorial Army units in the province as long as infantry units were not included.

With the worsening political situation in Europe, steps were quickly taken to form two units, 188th (Antrim) Heavy Battery RA (TA) and the Antrim Fortress Company RE (TA). The role of the latter was to operate the searchlights which had recently been installed at Grey Point and Kilroot, maintain the engines which provided power for the lights and also maintain the electrical equipment at both forts. Recruiting commenced in August 1937 and both units were briefly mobilised during the Munich crisis in 1938.

Until the mid-1930s there had been no major physical changes or improvements made to the defences of Belfast Lough. However, by 1935 the British government had begun to consider limited rearmament in the light of the country's improving economic situation and the rapid recovery of Germany, both politically and economically, under its new Chancellor, Adolf Hitler. At Grey Point and Kilroot little had been done to improve or modernise the forts in the years since they had been completed but now

Searchlight position at Grey Point Fort.   *Author*

some small improvements were authorised. The lack of searchlights had always been a limiting factor preventing the guns of both forts from being fought effectively by night. Now the decision was taken to provide two coast artillery searchlights for each fort and at Grey Point a new two-storey battery observation post was authorised, with a control post for the searchlights and a telephone room on the ground floor beneath the observation post. The two searchlight positions and the new observation post were completed in 1936.

Two 4.5-inch (115-mm) howitzers were also allocated to provide the mobile armament for the land-front defence and the following year the Belfast Defence Scheme was modified and plans introduced to mount two medium machine-guns at the seaward entrance to the docks. Once again East and West Twin Islands were selected as the sites for these weapons.

While the War Office was improving marginally the defences of Belfast Lough, the Admiralty was not idle. In the same year as the searchlights were installed in the forts, the Admiralty gave consideration to providing a controlled mining base at Belfast and a controlled minefield was planned between Carrickfergus Bank and Lobster Rock near Grey Point. The Royal Navy had assumed responsibility for submarine mining from the Royal Engineers in 1904 and the modern controlled minefields were the linear descendants of the Victorian submarine mines of 50 years earlier. Submarine mines were anchored in groups and detonated electrically beneath or close to a ship by an observer in a control post on the shore rather than by actual contact with the vessel. In Belfast Lough the control post for the minefield was planned to be at Grey Point Fort.

To counter the submarine menace the Admiralty also

Personnel of 9th HAA Regiment RA (SR) parading at their training centre in Londonderry shortly before the outbreak of war in 1939.
Londonderry Sentinel

planned to lay a B2 indicator net and loop between Black Head on the Antrim side of the lough and the South Briggs Rocks just off Orlock Point. A gap for shipping was provided approximately mid-way across the lough. The net and loop were designed to indicate the presence of any submarine attempting to enter the lough submerged, which would then be engaged by anti-submarine patrol boats.

By 1938, attack from the sea was no longer the sole threat to the United Kingdom. It was now necessary to defend the country against a new threat, that of air attack. This new threat, which had first been experienced during World War One, demanded its own specialised defensive measures, using a combination of fighter aircraft, anti-aircraft guns and searchlights. The bulk of the resources available for the defence of Great Britain were concentrated along the south and east coasts and around London. Northern Ireland, by the nature of its position at the extreme limit of the range, or indeed beyond the range, of most bomber aircraft then in service with continental air forces, was given the lowest priority for all forms of air defence. However, the Munich crisis had served to emphasise how ill prepared the British armed forces were and immediate steps were taken to increase

recruiting for the Territorial Army and the other reserves.

The two newly raised Territorial Army units were quickly recruited to full strength, but they were not the only volunteer units in Northern Ireland – they were soon followed by a number of units of the Supplementary Reserve. Normally personnel of the Supplementary Reserve were individual reservists with specialist skills required by the Army in time of war but not required in any number during peacetime. These reservists were frequently railwaymen, miners, electricians or signallers and were sometimes formed into units such as Royal Engineers railway companies or signal companies of the Royal Corps of Signals. All were part of the First Class Army Reserve. Northern Ireland was unique in providing a major unit of the Royal Armoured Corps, the North Irish Horse (SR), and a Royal Artillery brigade, 3rd Anti-Aircraft Brigade RA (SR). The latter comprised 8th (Belfast) HAA Regiment RA (SR), 9th (Londonderry) HAA Regiment RA (SR) and the 3rd (Ulster) Searchlight Regiment RA (SR) together with its affiliated minor units of the Royal Signals, RASC and RAOC. On mobilisation the brigade was to form part of the Army field force.

Northern Ireland's low priority for air defence meant that in 1939 the province held only a token quantity of equipment. Prior to the outbreak of war in September 1939 this equipment amounted to a total of 20 guns: 12 3-inch (75-mm) HAA guns and eight 40-mm LAA guns together with 32 searchlights. These guns and searchlights were used as the training equipment for the Supplementary Reserve anti-aircraft brigade. No anti-aircraft regiments were dedicated to the air defence of Northern Ireland but the approved total of guns to be provided when available was 24 HAA guns. However, the War Office agreed that although the 3rd Anti-Aircraft Brigade RA (SR) was designated for service with the field force, it would be made available for local air defence prior to its despatch overseas with the field force. In addition, the Admiralty pointed out that this limited defence could always be supplemented by the anti-aircraft guns of any naval escort vessels that might be in Belfast Lough or Lough Foyle at the time of an enemy attack. However, these arrangements were very ad hoc and scarcely constituted a coordinated air defence scheme so necessary if there was to be any form of effective defence against enemy air attack.

So when war broke out again with Germany on 3 September 1939, just over 20 years after the end of World War One, the defences of Belfast Lough were little changed from their state at the end of that war. Only the strategic situation had changed dramatically, with the return of the Treaty ports in the Irish Free State to Irish control. The vitally important escort bases of Queenstown (Cork) and Lough Swilly could no longer be used by the Royal Navy, making the defeat of the German submarine menace doubly difficult and vastly increasing the strategic value of bases in Northern Ireland.

12 World War Two – Part One 1939–1941

War is declared

The outbreak of war with Germany was a foregone conclusion once Germany invaded Poland on 1 September 1939 since Poland's borders, like Belgium's in 1914, had been guaranteed by Britain and France. From the time of the Munich crisis in 1938 the war clouds had been looming over Europe and the British government, realising reluctantly the increasing likelihood of war with Germany, had hastily instituted a belated rearmament programme for the armed forces. Naval shipbuilding and aircraft contracts increased the importance of Belfast in the eyes of the Admiralty and the Air Ministry but little was actually done to improve the defences against attack by sea or air, nor were additional units of the Territorial Army raised in the province as had been done in the rest of the United Kingdom.

The diplomatic situation began to deteriorate seriously in early 1939 when Hitler made clear his demands for access to the Free Port of Danzig which, prior to the Versailles Treaty of 1919, had been German. He also demanded an extra-territorial road and railway across Polish territory to link East and West Prussia. In March, German troops occupied the rump of Czechoslovakia, making it a German protectorate. The reaction of the British Prime Minister, Neville Chamberlain, was to announce in April the introduction of peace-time conscription. During the summer Britain moved steadily onto a war footing with the recall of reservists to the colours. However, it was the announcement of an impending non-aggression pact between Germany and Russia on 21 August that brought about the inevitability of war as it opened the way for Germany to strike at Poland without fear of Russian intervention.

The pact was actually signed by Germany and Russia on 24 August and on the same day the British Parliament, recalled from its summer recess, passed an Emergency Powers Bill giving almost unlimited authority to the government. Later that day, at 16.00

hours, the headquarters of 188th (Antrim) Heavy Battery RA (TA) at the drill hall in Great Victoria Street in Belfast received a telegram from the War Office ordering all coast defences to be manned at war routine as soon as possible. By 22.40 hours that evening Grey Point Fort was reported as fully manned and an infantry garrison was provided by a platoon from the Regular infantry battalion stationed at Palace Barracks, Holywood. Another platoon from the battalion at Victoria Barracks in Belfast was dispatched to Kilroot and by 09.30 hours on 25 August Kilroot Fort was also reported as being fully manned. Communication was opened with the Port War Signal station at Orlock Point and a searchlight normally used for training purposes was removed from the Drill Hall and installed at Kilroot. Belfast Lough Fixed Defences were ready for war.[1]

On 26 August the Admiralty requested the Board of Trade to commence War Watching Duties and on the same day the Coastguard at Donaghadee reported a German merchant vessel proceeding northwards, but as Britain and Germany were still at peace the ship was allowed to continue on its way without being stopped. In the next two or three days the Naval Liaison Officer, Lieutenant Commander H Watts RN, reported for duty at Grey Point together with two Royal Navy petty officers for recognition duty and three Royal Marine signallers for duty as Examination Service signallers.[2]

The Examination Service at Belfast was formally established on 2 September with Grey Point Fort acting as the examination battery. On the same day the Regular Army infantry platoon acting as garrison at Grey Point Fort was replaced by a detachment of the National Defence Corps. This detachment came from National Defence Corps companies which were raised between 1936 and 1939 by local TA Associations. The role of these companies was the defence of vulnerable points, and the personnel recruited into the companies all had previous war experience. Normally these companies

Manning the guns at Grey Point Fort in the closing months of 1939.   *Author's collection*

were affiliated to and administered by the local TA infantry battalions but in Northern Ireland there were no such battalions. Subsequently, after the outbreak of war, the National Defence Corps companies in Northern Ireland were absorbed into the Home Service infantry battalions.

At 13.40 hours on 3 September a further telegram was received from the War Office reading "War has broken out with Germany" and normal war routine at both forts was immediately established. No doubt excitement ran high in the first few days as the forts settled into the routine and prepared to do battle with the pocket battleships *Graf Spee* and *Deutschland*, both of which ships had been reported at sea since 20 August. Two days after the outbreak of war, the gunners at Grey Point Fort had their first, and indeed only, opportunity to fire almost in anger. At 08.15 hours on 5 September the small coasting steamer SS *E. Hayward* entered the lough quite unaware that war had been declared with Germany. When the vessel failed to respond to a recognition signal a plugged shell, that is a shell without its normal high explosive filling, was fired across her bows to bring her to. Rumour has it that the shell went on to hit a farm building near Kilroot Fort on the

opposite side of the lough.[3]

As the 188th (Antrim) Heavy Battery RA settled into war routine and training, by December 1939 the strength of the battery was 214 all ranks under the command of Lieutenant Colonel OB Graham, OC Fixed Defences Belfast Lough. The infantry platoon at Kilroot Fort was relieved by a second detachment of the National Defence Corps, and the increasing size of the battery and the requirement to man two separate forts brought about a change in the unit title on 1 March 1940. On that date the battery was reorganised as Antrim Heavy Regiment RA (TA) consisting of 188th Battery at Grey Point and the newly formed 200th Battery at Kilroot. Lieutenant Colonel Graham remained in command of the new regiment.

Although coast defence batteries provided only a small target to the guns of enemy ships, it was a different matter when it came to air attack. Defence against the threat from the air now became a very high priority and the decision was taken to protect coast defence guns by providing them with concrete overhead cover. Work started on constructing the concrete gun houses at both forts during the winter of 1939–40, and covers for the four gun positions were completed by

The 6-inch (152-mm) BL Mk VII guns at Grey Point with the concrete overhead protection provided in 1940. *Author*

June 1940. A rectangular-shaped concrete cover was built over each gun position to protect the guns and the immediate crew working area. The roof was 3 feet (0.92 metres) thick and was supported by concrete crossbeams. The entrance to the underground magazine, however, was not protected and remained vulnerable.

Active anti-aircraft defence was provided by the deployment of one 3-inch (75-mm) AA gun to each fort. The gun at Grey Point was mounted about 300 yards (275 metres) from the fort on the fairway of the second hole at Helen's Bay golf course. These two guns were for the immediate defence of the two forts and were integrated with the Belfast Lough Fixed Defences and were not under command of HQ AA Defences.

Threat of invasion, 1940–41

The crushing German blitzkreig in France and the resulting evacuation of the BEF from Dunkirk in May and early June 1940 brought to an end the so-called 'phony war'. Now Great Britain stood alone, threatened with invasion for the first time since Napoleon had concentrated his Grande Armee on the French Channel coast over 130 years before.

British strategy had been designed on the basis that the Royal Navy would have the active support of the French navy. Now, at a stroke, the Royal Navy had lost that support and was unexpectedly required to provide ships to defend British interests in the Mediterranean and to counter the modern Italian fleet now allied with the Germans.

The ability of the Germans to land troops in Norway in April 1940, albeit operating from nearby German naval bases, had come as a salutary lesson to both the Royal Navy and the British Army. Now that the Germans occupied the complete length of the coast of Europe from Oslo to Cherbourg it seemed that invasion was not just a possibility but almost a foregone conclusion.

Immediate steps were taken to fortify all commercial ports and possible landing beaches in the United

One of the 6-inch (152-mm) BL Mk VII naval gun at Magilligan Point in 1941. *Imperial War Museum*

Kingdom. New coast defence batteries known as 'emergency batteries' were established all along the coast using spare guns from Royal Artillery stocks and the large number of guns from ships scrapped under the Washington Naval Treaty that had been held in store in the Royal Navy dockyards. These emergency batteries usually comprised two guns, each protected by a concrete or brick gun house. A battery observation post was sited behind the guns and there was a protected magazine. The whole site was surrounded by a barbed wire fence and defended by a number of concrete pillboxes. Many of these batteries were sited to defend vulnerable beaches which were also defended with barbed wire, mines and concrete anti-tank obstacles.

Although the German plan for Operation Sealion, the code name for the invasion of England, was for a landing on the coasts of Kent and Sussex, it was still felt necessary to defend the main ports of Northern Ireland. Headquarters VI Corps, the major field force headquarters in the province, believed there were three potential threats to Northern Ireland: firstly, an airborne assault; secondly, a sea landing launched from bases in north-western France; or, thirdly, an attack through the Irish Free State by German forces which had landed on the Irish south or west coasts. De Valera was determined to keep the Irish Free State neutral in the developing conflict but, based on previous experience, there did not seem to be any reason why Hitler should respect that neutrality if it did not suit him to do so.

It was also necessary to defend the ports of Larne and Londonderry, and in providing the requisite armament for each port there then commenced what might be described as a game of musical guns which reflected the critical urgency of the situation even in Northern

Ireland. On 6 June 1940 one 12-pdr QF gun was mounted and ready for action at Larne manned by an officer and 13 other ranks from 200th Battery RA at Kilroot. Three weeks later this gun was moved to Ebrington Barracks in Londonderry and replaced at Larne by a 4.7-inch (120-mm) QF gun. By the end of June a naval 6-inch (152-mm) BL Mk VII gun on a naval P III mounting was also installed and ready for action at Larne, once again manned by a detachment from Kilroot.

It was clear that the 12-pdr QF gun at Ebrington Barracks in Londonderry could only provide defence against light craft or a submarine penetrating the entrance to Lough Foyle on the surface. There was an urgent need to improve the defences of the lough in view of its likely importance as a naval base and this was carried out as heavier guns became available. On 1 July two officers and 39 other ranks from the 188th Battery RA at Grey Point moved to Magilligan to man two 6-inch (152-mm) BL Mk VII guns on naval P III mountings, which were in the process of being installed beside the old Martello tower at the Point. By 5 July the guns at Magilligan Point were ready for action.

In June the Royal Artillery took over the operation of the searchlights, generating machinery and other electrical equipment from the Royal Engineers. This was the result of a War Office decision to increase the number of Royal Engineers field companies. So the Antrim Fortress Company RE relinquished its coast defence duties and, in October, concentrated at Kilroot for field engineer training prior to becoming a field company. However, 32 DEL Engine Room staff remained with the Fixed Defences. One result of the handover of the searchlights to the Royal Artillery was a change in terminology – searchlights were no longer officially termed Defence Electric Lights (DEL) but became Coast Defence Searchlights (CDSL). In early July two new coast defence searchlights were installed at Kilroot and one of the old searchlights from Kilroot was moved to Magilligan.[4]

On 14 July the title of the Antrim Heavy Regiment RA (TA) was changed to 525 (Antrim) Coast Regiment RA and ten days later 188th Battery and 200th Battery were designated 'A' and 'B' Batteries respectively. At the same time the guns at Larne were given battery status as 'C' Coast Battery RA while those at Magilligan became 'D' Coast Battery RA. The detachment at Ebrington Barracks became 'Z' Section RA. Ten days later 'C' Coast Battery was re-designated as 380th Coast Battery

RA and 'D' Coast Battery became 381st Coast Battery RA.[6]

While these changes in nomenclature were occurring, the ordnance merry-go-round continued. For the Royal Navy the priority was now to provide merchant vessels with guns. The Admiralty considered the most suitable gun for this role was the 4.7-inch (120-mm) QF gun and it began to recover all guns of this calibre that had initially been provided to arm emergency batteries such as the one at Larne. As a result of this policy a second 6-inch (152-mm) BL Mk VII on a naval P IV mounting was substituted on 25 July for the 4.7-inch (120-mm) QF gun at Larne. Both guns were sited close to Chaine's Tower beside the harbour, one gun at the end of Bay Road and the other to the right of the tower.

In August, elements of a third battery were established on the shores of Belfast Lough when another 6-inch (152-mm) BL gun on a naval P IV mounting was installed close to the Port War Signal Station on Orlock Point. Twenty-one other ranks were posted from 'A' Battery at Grey Point to man the Orlock gun. Finally, at the end of the month, the peripatetic 12-pdr QF gun was moved again, this time to become an integral part of 380th Coast Battery RA at Magilligan Point.[7]

The batteries at Larne and Orlock were also provided with concrete gun houses but at Magilligan it proved more difficult. As with the construction of the Martello tower over 100 years earlier, the problem was the provision of adequate foundations which proved extremely difficult in the sand. Nor was an attempt made to provide the 12-pdr QF gun with any form of overhead cover because of the problem of designing a gun house that would permit the gun to traverse through the required arc of 180 degrees.[5]

Installation of guns and searchlights continued until 31 January 1941 when by that date a second 6-inch (152-mm) BL gun on a naval P VIII mounting was in place at Orlock. The two guns were protected by concrete gun houses, and two brick coast artillery searchlight positions with armoured glass shutters were built on the rocks close to the edge of the sea. The Orlock battery, now known as 'C' Coast Battery RA, took over the duties of examination battery on 1 February from 'A' Coast Battery at Grey Point, and HQ Belfast Fire Command was also established close to the Port War Signal Station. A second searchlight was also installed at Magilligan Point.[8] However, there was a problem with the fire control of the emergency batteries. Unlike the permanent forts at Grey Point and Kilroot,

none of the new batteries were equipped with depression rangefinders. It was not until the middle of 1942 that a 12-foot (3.6-metre) Barr and Stroud FT 6 optical rangefinder was provided for each battery.

The Northern Ireland Fixed Defences were now complete and comprised a total of ten 6-inch (152-mm) BL guns, one 12-pdr QF gun and ten coast artillery searchlights. The two 3-inch (75-mm) 20-cwt AA guns mounted at Grey Point and Kilroot were no longer under the control of HQ Fixed Defences and had been taken over by HQ AA Defences in November 1940. In April 1941 there was a further re-designation of the batteries of 525th (Antrim) Coast Regiment RA with 'A', 'B' and 'C' Coast Batteries becoming 113th, 114th and 115th Coast Batteries RA respectively. Although an integral part of the Northern Ireland Fixed Defences, 380th and 381st Coast Batteries RA were not incorporated into 525th (Antrim) Coast Regiment RA until February 1942.

Despite being distant from those parts of the United Kingdom most threatened with invasion, Belfast Lough saw quite a lot of enemy air activity in the latter months of 1940. In July a single enemy aircraft flew over the lough dropping mines which resulted in the loss of the SS *Troutpool* on 20 July. Further mine laying took place on 24 July and on 4 August the HAA gun at Kilroot Fort engaged an enemy aircraft. On subsequent days Royal Navy minesweepers exploded mines in the lough. On 13 September an enemy aircraft dropped incendiaries over Bangor and on 26 September the HAA gun at Grey Point Fort was in action against another German aircraft. After that date enemy minelaying diminished although some mines were occasionally detonated by the minesweepers which regularly swept a cleared channel in the lough. However, in 1940, Belfast was spared the heavy air raids which other British cities were suffering.

Headquarters VI Corps, the major field force headquarters in Northern Ireland and HQ Northern Ireland District, along with other commands and districts in the United Kingdom, quickly prepared contingency plans for defence against attack from the sea and, in the case of Northern Ireland, attack from the Irish Free State. In June the 61st Infantry Division was moved to the province to reinforce the garrison which prior to the arrival of the division comprised only one armoured regiment (the North Irish Horse) and a number of infantry battalions. Two battalions – 5th Bn Royal Inniskilling Fusiliers and 6th Bn Royal Ulster Rifles – were Home Defence battalions, the latter

World War Two pillbox at Magilligan Point.   *Author*

Pillbox on the beach at Downhill, County Londonderry. This pillbox was constructed from black basalt stone obtained locally.
Author

having been formed from National Defence Corps companies. Both battalions comprised mainly older men and those in lower medical categories. Two other battalions – 5th Royal Irish Fusiliers and 7th Royal Ulster Rifles – were recruited on the basis of service only in Northern Ireland and one of their subsequent tasks was to provide garrisons for the batteries of the Fixed Defences.

By December 1940 another division, 53rd (Welsh) Infantry Division, had also been moved to Northern Ireland, coming under command of HQ VI Corps. In all, between mid-June and mid-December 1940 the total strength of the Army units in the province increased from 25,000 to 79,000 officers and men.

The military appreciation of the situation in late 1940 was that the north-west coast of Northern Ireland, where there were long stretches of open beach, was the most likely landing area for a German amphibious invasion force. The defence of the beaches at Magilligan, Portstewart, Portrush, Cushendun, Cushendall, Carnlough and Glenarm became the responsibility of 61st Infantry Division, and troops from the division immediately commenced fortifying them. This was done by constructing concrete pillboxes, anti-tank obstacles and barbed wire entanglements. At Magilligan the length of the beach was obstructed using wooden posts to prevent enemy aircraft from landing. Only two brigades of 61st Infantry Division were allocated to beach defence as one of the division's brigades was detailed to be prepared to act as a striking force. This brigade, reinforced by a regiment of field artillery and other units, was to secure Lough Swilly for use as a fleet anchorage by the Royal Navy if ordered to do so.[9]

At the other side of the province, in the south-east corner, the magnificent beaches of Tyrella Strand and Dundrum Bay, though considered less vulnerable to amphibious assault, were also fortified and the garrison provided by troops of 53rd (Welsh) Infantry Division. This division was deployed along the border with the Irish Free State in Down, Armagh and Fermanagh and was tasked with implementing Plan 'W'. This was a contingency plan to be implemented immediately German troops landed in the Irish Free State, and the division, supported by 148th Infantry Brigade, had the role of striking south to secure Dublin and the airfields at Collinstown and Baldonnell.[10]

Work quickly went ahead fortifying the beaches and siting pillboxes to defend them and the exits from the beaches along roads leading inland. The River Bann, from Portstewart on the coast to Toome on the shores of Lough Neagh, was used as the base for a major defence line, the Bann Line, and was defended with pillboxes along its length. Many, but not all, of these pillboxes conformed to the dozen or so standard designs produced by FW3, the branch of the War Office's Directorate of

A 3.7 in (93 mm) HAA gun on a mobile mounting. This was the standard HAA gun in use with the British Army during World War Two.   *Author's collection*

Fortifications and Works. Based on these designs the larger pillboxes were designed to hold two machine-guns or two light machine-guns and an anti-tank rifle while the smaller ones were to hold one light machine-gun and an anti-tank rifle.

Many other pillboxes, however, were designed to meet local needs and were built using local materials. At Downhill, near Magilligan, one pillbox was built of local black basalt while at Magilligan Point itself there was a unique two-storey concrete pillbox designed to engage an enemy on the beach whilst also providing observation and fire across Lough Foyle from its upper storey. Even Carrickfergus Castle had a brick pillbox constructed above the old Water Gate. It was somewhat ironic that despite the neutrality of the Irish Free State much of the cement used to make the concrete for the beach defences was bought from suppliers in that country.

In April 1941, 5th Infantry Division was moved to Northern Ireland and in the following month there was a rearrangement of the higher headquarters in the province. Headquarters VI Corps relinquished its field role and became instead Headquarters British Troops Northern Ireland (BTNI) while the field role was taken over by the newly arrived Headquarters III Corps, with 5th Infantry and 53rd (Welsh) Infantry Divisions under command. By this time the garrison also included one independent infantry brigade group and two independent infantry brigades. This large influx of troops meant that by April 1941 the Chief Engineer at HQ Northern Ireland District was working at full stretch to provide sufficient accommodation and 'Q' facilities to support them all. It was now that Northern Ireland came under serious attack for the first time in the war.

Air attack

The Supplementary Reserve anti-aircraft brigade was mobilised on 25 August 1939 and 8th (Belfast) HAA Regiment RA, together with elements of 9th (Londonderry) HAA Regiment, was immediately deployed to provide the anti-aircraft defence of Belfast. On mobilisation the regiments were armed with only a fraction of their war establishment of guns, a total of 12 3-inch (75-mm) 20-cwt AA guns, eight 40-mm LAA guns and 32 searchlights. However, the brigade did not remain as an entity for long as almost immediately 9th (Londonderry) HAA Regiment RA was sent to the Middle East while the remainder of the brigade moved to England to join the BEF.

The brigade headquarters returned to Northern Ireland after Dunkirk and took over the anti-aircraft defences of the province with 102nd HAA Regiment RA and 309th HAA Battery RA under command. The latter battery had arrived in November 1939 tasked with training 102nd HAA Regiment which was a Home Defence anti-aircraft regiment formed a few days before the outbreak of war. These two units were gradually armed with 3.7-inch (93-mm) HAA guns as they became available. There were two types of 3.7-inch (93-mm) HAA guns, the static and the mobile. The guns were virtually identical except that the mounting of the static model was fixed on a holdfast in a permanent gun pit while the mobile model was trailer-mounted and could be fired from temporary positions. These were more powerful guns than the older 3-inch (75-mm) 20-cwt AA guns which, although good, dated from World War One. These latter guns, which had been used as training guns for 3rd Anti-Aircraft Brigade, had been withdrawn and sent to England in the closing months of 1939.

In 1937 the anti-aircraft equipment approved for the defence of Northern Ireland by the Committee of Imperial Defence was one HAA regiment of three batteries, each of four mobile 3.7-inch (93-mm) HAA guns and two LAA batteries with a total of 24 40-mm

HAA gun position at Magilligan Point, County Londonderry.

Author

LAA guns. In addition the RAF was to provide a fighter squadron and a sector headquarters.[11] However, by the middle of 1940 the approved armament for the province had been increased to 24 3.7-inch (93-mm) HAA guns in six four-gun sites and 26 40-mm LAA guns in single-gun positions. In fact, in early May 1940 the number of guns actually in position totalled four static 3.7-inch (93-mm) HAA guns, three mobile HAA guns of the same calibre, and two 40-mm LAA guns but there were no searchlights. The RAF had four fighter aircraft based at RAF Aldergrove, near Antrim, none of which were allocated for the defence of Belfast but which probably could be used for this role, if necessary.

Permanent HAA sites were usually built for batteries of four guns and by 1941 there was a standard layout which consisted of a command post, usually located at the centre of the site, four gun pits and at least one magazine. Accommodation for the battery personnel was in Nissen huts while the command post and magazine were almost always low single-storey concrete or brick buildings surrounded by earth banks. Each gun pit consisted of a concrete base with a holdfast for the gun placed centrally. The base was surrounded by a concrete blast wall about five feet (1.53 metres) high and was frequently octagonal in shape, though other patterns were used depending on the geography of the site. Within the gun pits there were built-in ammunition lockers and crew shelters protected by steel doors. All the gun pits and other buildings were linked by a concrete service road. All HAA battery sites in the United Kingdom were identified by one or more letters and a number and the Belfast sites were prefixed with the letter 'U' while those around Londonderry used the letters 'LO'.

The first battery site to be established by 102nd HAA Regiment RA was a four-gun site with static HAA guns at Kinnegar on the outskirts of Holywood. This site, allotted the designation U 1, was followed soon after by a second HAA site, U 3, at Lisnabreeny on the south-eastern outskirts of Belfast. This second battery was for three 3.7-inch (93-mm) mobile HAA guns. However, the withdrawal of British forces from the continent speeded up the allocation of anti-aircraft guns for the defence of Northern Ireland. Between June and December 1940 two more battery sites, U 4 and U 6, became operational and U 3 received a fourth gun. Three 3-inch (75-mm) 20-cwt AA guns were acquired from the Royal Navy and were sited in the Belfast harbour area between East Twin Island and the Belfast power station. These three guns were manned by personnel of 175th and 176th LAA Batteries RA and in November these batteries also took over the manning of the AA guns previously allotted to the Fixed Defences.

Two HAA gun sites were also established in and around Londonderry, LO 1 east of the River Foyle at Corrody and LO 2 at Shantallow on the west bank of the river. These four-gun sites were manned by 315th HAA Battery RA, from 102nd HAA Regiment, and a fourth battery, 431st HAA Battery RA, which had been moved to Northern Ireland on temporary duty to make 102nd HAA Regiment up to a four-battery regiment.

By the end of 1940, Headquarters 3rd Anti-Aircraft Brigade had under command, in addition to 102nd HAA Regiment RA, one LAA regiment, 66th LAA Regiment RA, but there were no searchlight regiments. In early 1941, 146th (Z) Battery RA was moved to Northern Ireland. This unit was equipped with 12 nine-barrelled rocket projectors firing 3-inch (75-mm) unrotated projectiles or rockets. These projectiles had a ceiling of 22,000 feet (6,760 metres) with a warhead similar in weight to that of a 3.7-inch (93-mm) HAA shell. The equipment was simple to install and operate and was used to reinforce the defences of large towns.

Although there were few fighter aircraft to spare for Northern Ireland in 1940 the RAF did take steps to establish a balloon defence for Belfast and Londonderry. One balloon squadron, No 968 Squadron RAF, was deployed from Scotland for the defence of Belfast and Belfast Lough. The squadron comprised five flights each of eight balloons, and one flight was waterborne and deployed off Bangor. A second squadron, No 920 Squadron RAF, with three flights, provided the balloon defence for Londonderry.

This was the state of the Northern Ireland anti-aircraft

Troops clearing debris in Belfast after the German air raid on the night of 15/16 April 1941.   *Belfast Telegraph*

defences in early 1941 and the weakness of the defences was well known to the German High Command as Luftwaffe reconnaissance aircraft had carried out a number of photographic missions over Belfast and Londonderry in late 1940. By the early spring of 1941 both Glasgow and Liverpool had suffered a number of heavy air raids and on the night of 7/8 April it was the turn of Belfast to be attacked. On that night there was a small-scale air raid on Belfast carried out by six enemy aircraft, and parachute mines and incendiary bombs were dropped on the harbour area. These caused a major fire in a timber yard close to the docks while a parachute mine caused the destruction of the Harland and Wolff fuselage factory where fuselages for 50 Stirling bombers were in the course of construction. Despite the feebleness of the anti-aircraft barrage the enemy aircraft did not escape unscathed, as one Heinkel He 111 was destroyed over Downpatrick in County Down by a Hurricane fighter of

245 Fighter Squadron RAF based at Aldergrove.

The raid on 7/8 April was clearly designed to test the Belfast defences. A week later, on the night of 15/16 April, the Luftwaffe returned in strength when 180 aircraft approached the city from the south-east at 22.40 hours before the moon had risen. The German aircraft were engaged by the guns of the anti-aircraft defences reinforced by the 4.5-inch (114-mm) dual purpose guns and the multiple 2-pdr Pom Poms of HMS *Furious* which was under repair in one of Harland and Wolff's docks. The efficacy of the anti-aircraft fire was diminished by the lack of searchlights, and effective resistance virtually ceased when a large bomb exploded next to the central telephone exchange and severed most of the telephone lines including those linking Belfast with England and Scotland. This affected the RAF Fighter Sector Headquarters which lost its link with the control centres in Britain and, to make matters worse, communications were also lost between the Gun Operations Control Room at Headquarters 3rd Anti-Aircraft Brigade and the guns. As a result, all anti-aircraft fire virtually ceased altogether.

The German aircraft dropped 200 tons of high explosive bombs and 800 canisters of incendiaries. However, most of the damage was to civilian property in the area of the Waterworks and the reservoirs in the north of the city which the Luftwaffe navigators may have mistaken for the harbour area. The total of those killed in the air raid was over 700, considerably more than were killed in Coventry during the raid of 14 November 1940.[12] While Belfast was bearing the brunt of the German attack, Londonderry, Bangor and Newtownards did not escape. Two parachute mines were dropped on Londonderry killing 15 people and five more died when another mine fell on Bangor. Damage to Newtownards was confined to the airfield. Although no claims of hits on enemy aircraft were made by the anti-aircraft gunners, German sources admitted that five of their aircraft failed to return to their bases.

The largest air raid on Belfast came in the early hours of the morning of the 5 May when the Luftwaffe returned in even greater strength. In a period of four hours 200 bombers dropped over 200 tons of high explosive bombs and more than 2,000 canisters of incendiaries on the city. By the time of this raid a searchlight battery had been moved to Northern Ireland from England and two other batteries were formed from personnel being trained in the province. The anti-aircraft batteries fired over 3,000 rounds of HAA ammunition but once again no hits on enemy aircraft were claimed by the gunners. It was left to another Hurricane, also from 245 Fighter Squadron RAF, to obtain the only 'kill' of the night when it destroyed a Junkers Ju 88 bomber over Ardglass.

On this occasion the German bombers had greater success in damaging the docks, shipyards, the harbour power station and the Short and Harland aircraft factory. Damage to Harland and Wolff was extensive and production was cut by 90% for ten days – it was almost six months before production returned to normal.

A number of ships under construction or being repaired were severely damaged and more than 200 people were killed, bringing the total loss of life in the three air raids to more than 900. On the following night, 6 May, there was a final light raid on Belfast and that was the last occasion on which the Luftwaffe attacked Northern Ireland.

After the May raids immediate steps were taken to increase the strength of the anti-aircraft defences of Northern Ireland and two HAA regiments were quickly dispatched from the United Kingdom. The first regiment, 111th HAA Regiment RA, arrived in mid-May and was closely followed by 1st HAA Regiment RA in June. The former was equipped with static guns but the latter was a mobile regiment. Work continued on the construction of new HAA gun sites with emphasis on the defence of the three main ports, Belfast, Londonderry and Larne, and the seaplane base at Lough Erne. At the same time large numbers of gun towers for single 40-mm LAA guns were erected at each of the new airfields now becoming operational in the province.

The year 1941 had been a difficult one for the people of the United Kingdom, and the inhabitants of Northern Ireland had shouldered their share of the hardships and casualties with the rest of the British population. Although there was no conscription in Northern Ireland, the province was now fully on a war-footing, its shipyards and factories turning out war materiel and its countryside providing a base and facilities for a corps headquarters and the equivalent of four infantry divisions. The Fixed Defences and the Anti-Aircraft Defences were now properly established and equipped but with the German invasion of Russia in the summer, the immediate threat of invasion of Britain or the Irish Free State was lifted. Any respite, however, was short-lived and ended by the treacherous attacks by the Japanese on Pearl Harbour, Hong Kong and Singapore in December. Another enemy had entered the war but the Japanese entry on the side of the Axis powers resulted in an ally for the hard-pressed British – the United States of America.

13 World War Two – Part Two 1942–1945

1942

By 1942 Northern Ireland had become a vital part of the defence of the United Kingdom. With the German occupation of France, all convoys were now routed around the north of Ireland to major west coast ports such as Glasgow, Liverpool and Swansea. Now that the Royal Navy no longer had the use of Lough Swilly as a naval base, Lough Foyle became critically important as a base for anti-submarine escort vessels while Belfast Lough became a convoy assembly location and a trawler base. At the same time as the Royal Navy was building up the size of its anti-submarine force in the province, the Army garrison also increased in strength with the arrival of the first elements of the American V Corps, and the Royal Air Force and the Fleet Air Arm were operating from more than a dozen new airfields.

At the start of 1942 the main British Army garrison in Northern Ireland continued to be Headquarters III Corps with two divisions – the 5th Infantry Division and the 59th Infantry Division – under its command. A third division, the 61st Infantry Division, came directly under the command of British Troops Northern Ireland (BTNI). The 5th Infantry Division left for England in January in order to make room for the first American division, the 34th (US) Infantry Division, which arrived in Londonderry in the same month and which was followed in February by the 1st (US) Armoured Division. These were the first American troops to go overseas to fight Hitler and were warmly welcomed in Northern Ireland. However, the use of the province as a training base for the Americans was strongly opposed by the Irish Taoiseach, de Valera, who believed their arrival constituted a violation of theoretical Irish sovereignty over Northern Ireland.

An American anti-aircraft regiment (actually a brigade of three battalions) also arrived at this time. The 209th Coast Artillery Regiment (Anti-aircraft) took over the manning of five HAA battery positions around Londonderry while the regiment awaited the arrival of its own guns. One of the battalions took over 16 40-mm LAA

guns from the War Office training pool and provided the air defence for four airfields: Limavady, Eglinton, Aldergrove and Nutts Corner.

Although by mid-1942 the fear of invasion was receding, Plan 'W' was still a current operational plan. This was the plan to counter a German invasion of the Irish Free State by securing Dublin and its airfields using a striking force mounted by the garrison in Northern Ireland. By June the number of major British formations in the province had been reduced to two, the 59th and the 61st Infantry Divisions, and for a short time the striking force became an Allied force comprising the 59th Infantry Division and the 34th (US) Infantry Division, both under the command of Headquarters V (US) Corps. The second British division, the 61st Infantry Division, was retained for the defence of Northern Ireland while the 1st (US) Armoured Division became the BTNI reserve.[1]

By this stage in the war it was assumed that in the unlikely event of a German attack on Ireland, entry into the Irish Free State by an Anglo-American force would be with the approval and cooperation of the Irish Free State government. Therefore, a liaison mission, the 18th Military Mission, was established and held ready to move to Dublin where it would be located at the Defence Forces GHQ. The Irish Free State Defence Forces also allocated Irish army liaison officers who were to be attached to the Anglo-American striking force as soon as it crossed the border into the Irish Free State.

In 1942 there were also changes in the organisation of the anti-aircraft defences in Northern Ireland. The 3rd Anti-Aircraft Brigade became the 7th Anti-Aircraft Group in September as a result of a re-organisation within Anti-Aircraft Command. As a result of this reorganisation, there was a reduction in the number of headquarters in the Command thus providing a much needed saving in manpower. A further saving was achieved by the introduction of ATS girls into newly formed 'mixed' HAA regiments where they took over many of the control duties

Personnel of 1st HAA Regiment RA training for their mobile role in Plan 'W'. The troops are manning a 3.7-inch (93-mm) HAA Mk IIIL gun while on exercise near Comber, County Down in 1942.

Imperial War Museum

previously undertaken by men. In the same month as the new anti-aircraft group was formed, the anti-aircraft defences of Northern Ireland were at their strongest with a total of 96 HAA guns, 48 LAA guns and 12 multi-barrelled 'Z' projectors in the province. These guns were deployed in three British HAA regiments, one British LAA regiment, one American Coast Artillery anti-aircraft regiment of three battalions, and two independent Coast Artillery anti-aircraft battalions.[2]

In October the Americans ceased to man any anti-aircraft positions in Northern Ireland and took over the mobile role in support of the striking force. To replace the Americans in the Londonderry static positions another British HAA regiment, the 126th HAA Regiment RA, was moved to Northern Ireland from England, bringing the total of HAA regiments to four. At the same time the decision was taken to set up two new four-gun anti-aircraft battery positions to protect the convoy anchorage in Belfast Lough. One position, BA1, was sited at Whitehead while the second, BA2, was on the other side of the lough on Ballymacormick Point, between Bangor and

Groomsport. While the primary role of these guns was the engagement of hostile aircraft in defence of the convoy anchorage, they were allotted a secondary role of engaging enemy shipping. In their secondary role, targets were to be engaged under the operational orders of OC Fixed Defences at Grey Point Fort.[3]

Two searchlights, one at Luke's Point in Bangor and one at Whitehead, also had a secondary CASL role in support of the Fixed Defences while another searchlight at Ballymacormick Point acted as a 'fighting light' or movable beam covering the water between Ballymacormick Point and Orlock Point. These guns and searchlights also covered the gap in the boom defence which was close to Ballymacormick Point.

Although the anti-aircraft guns with a secondary anti-shipping role at the entrance to Belfast Lough were the only additions to the armament of the Fixed Defences, a change had occurred in the manning of the five batteries. Aware of the need to make manpower savings even before the arrival of the 'mixed' HAA regiments, Lieutenant Colonel OB Graham, OC Fixed Defences, was determined to use ATS personnel to operate rangefinders, range transmitters and searchlights. Supported by the senior ATS officer in Northern Ireland, who was also his wife, he sought and obtained the necessary War Office authority and the 525th Coast Regiment RA became the only coast defence regiment in the Army where female personnel were employed in operational roles.

Throughout 1942 Northern Ireland's main contribution to the war came in providing bases for ships and aircraft involved in the Battle of the Atlantic. Additional airfields were completed until the number being used by the Royal Air Force and the United States Army Air Force totalled 26. This statistic was, in itself, a further indication of the vital importance of the province. Northern Ireland continued to provide bases and training facilities for the British and American armies until the whole province became an enormous armed camp. However, the tide of war was beginning to turn as the German advance on Egypt stalled at El Alamein and at Stalingrad in Russia. This change in the military fortunes of the Allies was to have a considerable effect on the level of defences in Northern Ireland.

The road to victory, 1943–45

The year 1943 opened on a brighter note for the Allies. It was now clear that though the war was not yet won there was no longer the likelihood that it might be lost. In the late autumn of 1942 a steady reduction in the size of the Army garrison in Northern Ireland commenced with the departure of the V (US) Corps to take part in the North African landings, and the corps was not immediately replaced by more American troops.

By early 1943 it was apparent that the Battle of the Atlantic was being won, due in a large part to the increasing use being made of bases in Northern Ireland and to the number of ships and aircraft operating out of them. That year the decision was taken by the Admiralty to base ocean escort groups of frigates at Belfast in place of the trawlers of the Irish Sea Escort Force which were transferred to Milford Haven and to establish an auxiliary training base for escort vessels at Larne.[4] The Royal Navy also set up a gun range at the Gobbins on Islandmagee near Larne. There Merchant Navy personnel, soldiers and Royal Marines from armed merchant ships were able to carry out practice firing with 4.7-inch (120-mm) QF and 12-pdr QF guns.

The Royal Air Force also was having increasing success against U-boats as more aircraft with greater range became available to support the convoys. By now there were ten Coastal Command squadrons based in the province and operating from airfields at Aldergrove, Ballykelly, Limavady and Lough Erne and air defence of these airfields and the naval bases assumed increased importance.

The major problem facing the Army in 1943 was manpower, and every effort was being made to keep the front-line divisions up to strength. However, this problem was alleviated by the fact that it was apparent that the German navy could no longer present a surface threat to the United Kingdom and that its offensive capability was now limited to submarine warfare. Similarly there was a marked reduction in the number of air attacks on the United Kingdom by the Luftwaffe, whose main theatre of operations was now the Russian front. As a result the War Office authorised a reduction in the size of the infantry garrison and ordered a review of the manning of both the Fixed Defences and the Anti-Aircraft Defences.

In February and March the 61st Infantry Division, the longest-serving formation in Northern Ireland, and the 59th Infantry Division left to be replaced by a single division, the 45th Infantry Division. At the same time Headquarters III Corps closed in Northern Ireland and also moved to England, leaving all remaining troops firstly under the command of BTNI and then, when that headquarters was closed, under Headquarters Northern Ireland District.

In Great Britain steps had been taken as early as 1942 to reduce the number of coastal defence batteries, and 50 batteries not directly guarding ports or harbours were abandoned while the manning of others was transferred to the Home Guard. In August 1943 the Northern Ireland coast defences were reviewed and the decision was taken to reduce the defences of Belfast Lough from three batteries to two by putting the guns at Grey Point into a state of care and maintenance. This was a logical decision since the battery at Orlock Point could do everything and more from its position at the entrance to the lough that the fort at Grey Point could do. Orlock was retained as the examination battery, and the Fire Command Post also remained at Orlock with the command post for the Royal Navy Extended Defence Officer. This latter officer controlled an electrically operated minefield laid at the entrance to the lough. The batteries at Larne and Magilligan Point were also retained as they too acted as examination batteries. In December the battery at Grey Point Fort was placed on a care and maintenance basis and the fort was now only used as the headquarters of the 525th (Antrim) Coast Regiment RA and as a naval signal station.

The anti-aircraft defences were also scaled down at this time. Although German air attacks on Belfast and Londonderry were still a possibility, the province was now much better equipped to counter any such attacks than it had been in April and May 1941. In July 1941 the Royal Air Force had established a separate Fighter Command group, No 82 Group, with three sector stations and responsibility for the operational control of all fighter squadrons in Northern Ireland. Three additional fighter squadrons were dispatched from England at the same time to reinforce the two squadrons already there.

These fighter squadrons were to remain until 1944 but the Army anti-aircraft defences began to be scaled down and economies made by reducing the number of HAA regiments from four to three. Two of these were 'mixed' regiments with a large number of ATS personnel integral to their establishments. The status of a number of four-gun sites was reduced from that of a battery to a troop, with a consequent manpower saving amongst the battery headquarters personnel. Included in these sites were BA1 at Whitehead and BA2 at Ballymacormick Point near Bangor. Additionally, the anti-aircraft units were able to release full-time personnel for service overseas by making use of the Ulster Home Guard. In September 1943 the Home Guard took over the night manning of two HAA batteries and in the following January took over full operational control of 16 guns on seven sites around Belfast and four guns at two sites at Londonderry.[5]

There was a brief surge in the strength of the garrison in the final months of 1943 and early 1944 when the XV (US) Corps consisting of three infantry divisions together with the famous 82nd Airborne Division arrived in preparation for D-Day. All these divisions were earmarked for the Normandy landings with the 2nd (US) Infantry Division and the 82nd (US) Airborne Division scheduled to land on D-Day and the remaining two divisions, the 5th (US) Infantry Division and the 8th (US) Infantry Division, as part of the follow-up force.

Even as the American force practised for D-Day, closures of anti-aircraft sites continued apace during 1944. At Magilligan Point the HAA battery site, LO7, was closed in February and in the same month BA1 at Whitehead was given up. In March the remaining HAA sites around Londonderry were closed and in April it was the turn of BA2 at Ballymacormick Point to be abandoned. With the departure of the units manning these sites, 188th (M) HAA Regiment RA and the 434th (Independent) HAA Battery RA, only one HAA and one LAA regiment remained in Northern Ireland. These regiments were not to remain for very long. By mid-summer the War Office had taken the decision to remove all the anti-aircraft defences from the province and in August the 7th Anti-Aircraft Group was disbanded and the last two regiments, the 141st (M) HAA Regiment RA and the 144th LAA Regiment RA, moved to England.

In July the 45th Infantry Division also left for England leaving behind one of its brigades as the sole remaining field force formation in the garrison which two years earlier had comprised a corps of three divisions. Only the Fixed Defences remained in operation and their days were also numbered. At the end of August the Admiralty decided to abolish the Examination Service at all ports in the United Kingdom and so examination batteries were no longer required. The four operational coast batteries were gradually run down, the majority of the personnel of the regiment were posted away and there only remained a small number with each battery responsible for the care and maintenance of the guns. The regiment continued in skeleton form until August 1945 when Lieutenant Colonel Graham DSO, OBE, who had commanded the Fixed Defences since the outbreak of war, was also posted out and the regiment was placed in a state of suspended animation.

Lough Swilly in 'The Emergency', 1939–45

The 'Emergency' was the term, almost a euphemism, which was used by the Irish Free State government to refer to the state of alert maintained by the country and its armed forces throughout the period of World War Two. Impoverished by the financial cost incurred in fighting the civil war that followed Irish independence in 1922, the Irish government felt unable to spend more than the minimum sum necessary to keep the Defence Forces in existence. As a result, de Valera found himself in the position of endeavouring to maintain a position of strict

An Irish Army 9.2-inch (233-mm) BL gun belonging to the Templebreedy battery at Cork carrying out a practice shoot during 'the Emergency'. The Lenan Head guns were virtually identical.   *Military Archives, Cathal Brugha Barracks, Dublin*

neutrality for the country with a small, ineffective army and virtually no air force or navy.

In 1939 the army was given authority to expand to a two-brigade organisation from a total of 6,000 regular troops. This total was actually 65% below the authorised establishment. The army lacked tanks, anti-aircraft guns, anti-tank guns, mortars and modern radios but the coast defence batteries, recently handed over by Great Britain under the terms of the revised treaty, were probably better equipped than any other branch of the army. Nor was the air force or the new Marine Service any better equipped than the army. The air force had only a handful of obsolescent fighters and light bombers while the total strength of the Marine Service was only six new MTBs and two old converted patrol vessels.

However, the terms of the handover of the Treaty ports by Great Britain included a clause that required the Irish Free State government to maintain the fortifications in good order. This necessitated the formation of new units of the Volunteer Reserve, a reserve force similar to the British Territorial Army, which was formed in 1934 and which, like the Territorial Army, was a part-time force. The Coastal Defence Artillery Volunteer Reserve was formed to man six new batteries, each of which had a cadre of regular personnel because of the technical nature

of the heavy guns. As we have seen, the batteries formed to man the Lough Swilly forts were the 5th Coast Artillery Battery at Fort Dunree and the 6th Coast Artillery Battery at Fort Lenan. Volunteers were recruited locally in Donegal and were mobilised for the duration of the war.

It was quite clear to the Defence Forces' planners that the strategic position of the Irish Free State meant that it was vulnerable to attack by both Great Britain and Germany. Britain needed the Treaty ports which had been returned only the previous year and which were vital in the battle against the German U-boat menace. For the Germans, occupation of Ireland would give them a base for attacks on the north-western ports of Britain and Hitler remarked that possession of Ireland would mean the end of England.[6] So plans were prepared to enable the Defence Forces to meet an attack by the British from Northern Ireland or landings by the Germans in the south or west.

The Irish Defence Forces were well aware that the British had a contingency plan to occupy the Inishowen Peninsula using troops from Northern Ireland, possibly supported by a seaborne landing. Equally the British were aware of the limited forces likely to oppose them. Indeed, the British Army intelligence estimate of the

Searchlight in its emplacement in the old fort at Dunree.

Author

strength of the Inishowen garrison appears to have been remarkably accurate. The strength of the two Lough Swilly forts was put at 278 all ranks including personnel of the Corps of Engineers Coastal Defence Company.[7] This company had its headquarters at Fort Camden in Cork harbour and was responsible for manning the searchlights, engines and generators in all the coastal defence forts, except Fort Lenan where there were no searchlights.

The British Intelligence estimate of the strength of the forts was extremely accurate as there was a garrison of 150 at Fort Dunree and 120 at Fort Lenan. The total for the Dunree garrison included personnel of the Fire Command headquarters and the Port Control organisation. This latter organisation was set up at the start of the 'Emergency' to control the movement of shipping in the lough and equated to the Examination Service in Great Britain. British Intelligence also correctly identified an infantry battalion as part of the

garrison. This battalion, the 17th Infantry Battalion, was the only battalion in Donegal and was based with its headquarters and one company at Letterkenny, companies at Buncrana, Finner and Rathmullen, and a detached platoon at Malin. All troops in Donegal came under the command of Headquarters Western Command.

In Dublin, GHQ plans for defence against invasion did not envisage the garrison of Inishowen being able to put up much more than a token defence against a determined British attack. The army was particularly short of ammunition for the coast defence guns: in March 1940 the number of rounds of ammunition available amounted to 170 rounds for each 9.2-inch (233-mm) gun and 275 rounds for each 6-inch (152-mm) gun. This meant that firing practice with full calibre rounds had to be severely restricted. It was not until July 1940, almost two years after the handover of the forts, that the first full-charge firing practice was carried out by 5th Coast Battery at Dunree. On that occasion the target launch *General McHardy* was brought round from Berehaven to tow the targets. After that, full-charge firing practice was carried out each year until 1945 but very few rounds could be fired.

Nor could the 17th Infantry Battalion be expected to oppose seriously the modern British forces since it was equipped only with small arms, 12 .303-inch (7.6-mm) Vickers medium machine-guns, and one or two 81-mm mortars. So the battalion was instructed to resist any invasion for as long as it could and then to revert to guerrilla warfare. This latter instruction rather emphasised the fact that the senior officers in Dublin, who had fought against the British in the War of Independence from 1919 to 1922, had very little conception how times had changed since then. The open moorland of Donegal did not lend itself to successful guerrilla operations against a modern enemy with command of the air.

Throughout the 'Emergency' the Defence Force was faced with the problem of acquiring modern equipment. Great Britain was the preferred source for military equipment but Britain needed every gun, shell and aircraft the country could produce. Also the British government was reluctant to provide arms and equipment that might, conceivably, be used against its own troops. One particular shortage was that of anti-aircraft guns and none were available for the protection of the forts. Understandably, the eight HAA guns and four LAA guns, which in 1940 comprised the equipment of the army's only anti-aircraft regiment, were concentrated for the

Irish army personnel manning a .303-inch (7.6-mm) Lewis light machine-gun on an AA mounting on Dunree Redoubt in 1942.
Military Archives, Cathal Brugha Barracks, Dublin

defence of Dublin and the airfields at Baldonnell and Collinstown. Before 1938 the British Army had decided against providing any anti-aircraft defence for the forts of Lough Swilly on the grounds that, at that time, the lough was out of range of land-based aircraft and was an unlikely target for seaborne aircraft.

However, by 1940 the situation had changed and now an attack by either German or British forces was a distinct possibility, bringing with it the dangers of air attack. Nevertheless, even when the acquisition of a number of additional anti-aircraft guns allowed some to be deployed to defend Cork harbour and Rineanna airfield on the Shannon, there were still no guns available for Lough Swilly. The only anti-aircraft weapons that could be provided for the forts were machine-guns. At Dunree some .303-inch (7.6-mm) Vickers medium

machine-guns and Lewis light machine-guns were mounted on anti-aircraft mountings on the upper fort, but even the height of Dunree Hill was insufficient to enable them to engage any but low-flying enemy aircraft. Surprisingly, no effort was made to provide the Lough Swilly guns with any form of physical protection from air attack. Unlike the British guns across the border, the Irish guns were only provided with light steel overhead shields despite the fact that, as the German raids on Belfast showed, the forts were well within the range of German as well as British bombers.

Between 1940 and 1945 little occurred to disturb the tranquillity of Lough Swilly other than the occasion when an Allied aircraft in trouble was forced to jettison a bomb which fell close to the village of Malin at the northern end of the Inishowen Peninsula.[8] Mines were occasionally washed ashore when they came loose from their moorings in storms but it was the constant Allied aircraft activity which provided the most drama. In the course of the war the garrisons at Dunree and Lenan had to attend to the salvage of more than 20 Allied aircraft which crashed on the wrong side of the Free State border or in the sea around the Donegal coast.

After the war the immediate and dramatic reduction in the strength of the Defence Forces meant that of the nine coast defence forts and batteries only two – Fort Westmoreland in Cork harbour and Fort Dunree – remained operational, though with their garrisons considerably reduced. In 1946, Fort Lenan was placed in care and maintenance with only a caretaker in residence and the fort was finally abandoned in 1952.

EPILOGUE

The post-war years

With the end of the war in Europe in May 1945 the emergency coast defence batteries at Orlock Point, Larne and Magilligan Point were quickly dismantled and the anti-aircraft sites abandoned and allowed to become derelict. The two permanent forts at Grey Point and Kilroot were retained in a state of care and maintenance under the supervision of 270th Independent Maintenance Battery RA while the War Office considered their future. By 1947 the decision had been taken to retain the permanent coast defence batteries throughout the United Kingdom and to man them using the personnel of new Royal Artillery coast regiments of the Territorial Army. In Northern Ireland the new coast regiment, the 429th (Antrim) Coast Regiment RA (TA), was formed in 1947. The first commanding officer of the regiment was Lieutenant Colonel EDR Shearer OBE, TD. Colonel Shearer was a noted amateur sportsman, having played football for both the Corinthians and England and cricket for Ireland. He and his successor, Lieutenant Colonel BD Cotton OBE, TD, had both served with 188th Heavy Battery RA (TA) and 525th Coast Regiment RA during the war.

The new regiment was entirely manned by volunteers as the National Service Acts did not apply to Northern Ireland, hence there were no National Servicemen completing their period of reserve service in the regiment. There was a small cadre of Regular Army personnel and the regiment was part of the 105th Coast Brigade RA based in Scotland. Initially the regiment comprised Regimental Headquarters and three batteries: 'P', 'R' and 'S' Batteries based at Carrickfergus and Belfast. In 1954 a fourth battery, 'Q', was formed. The regiment took over the forts at Grey Point and Kilroot but, unlike its predecessor, the 525th Coast Regiment RA, it was also equipped with mobile guns.

At Carrickfergus, P Battery was equipped with a towed version of the twin 6-pdr QF gun while S Battery in Belfast had 3.7-inch (93-mm) HAA guns which were used in the surface role. Both batteries were equipped with dispersed light searchlights and Universal rangefinders. The role of the dispersed light searchlights was to illuminate an area of water to enable the guns to engage targets while they were in the illuminated area rather than following the target with the beam. The second battery in Belfast, R Battery, manned the 6-inch (152-mm) BL guns at Grey Point and Kilroot where the equipment remained largely as it had been during the war. The only improvement made to these batteries was the modernisation of the method of range finding by the introduction of an anti-aircraft radar into each fort. The equipment was the Radar AA No 3 Mk 2/7, and in Grey Point Fort it was positioned on a ramp situated where the original battery command post had been sited.

Even this limited modernisation of the fire control of the guns was too little too late. The vast development of air power, guided missiles and, ultimately, the atomic bomb meant that at a time when the War Office was under intense pressure to make financial savings it was very difficult to justify the retention of the coast artillery. The radars were installed in 1954 and less than two years later, on 17 February 1956, the Ministry of Defence announced in the House of Commons the end of coast artillery. On 31 August 1956 the 429th Coast Regiment RA (TA) ceased to exist and the name and traditions of the Antrim Artillery were transferred to the newly-formed 146th Field Engineer Regiment RE (TA) together with the officers and men. In 1961 there was a further change of title when the regiment became the 74th (Antrim Artillery) Engineer Regiment RE (Volunteers) and it was finally disbanded in 1998.

On 3 January 1957 the 270th Independent Maintenance Battery RA was also disbanded and on the previous day the accommodation at Kilroot Fort had been handed over to the staff of the 21st Married Families Hostel. Soon work was in hand to remove the guns for scrap and the hutted accommodation at the rear of Grey Point Fort was taken over by Headquarters 39th Infantry Brigade, the garrison brigade in Northern Ireland. In the mid-1960s Kilroot Fort was sold for commercial development and the site built over.

At Lough Swilly a similar run-down in the garrisons of

Gunners of 429th Coast Regiment RA (TA) firing a 3.7-inch (93-mm) HAA gun in the coast defence role. The photograph was taken shortly before the regiment was disbanded in 1954.

Belfast Telegraph

the two forts occurred with the ending of the 'Emergency' and by the end of 1945 the combined strength of both forts had been reduced to 70 all ranks. The following year the order was given for the closure of all the coast defence forts with the exception of Fort Westmoreland on Spike Island in Cork harbour and Fort Dunree, so Lenan Fort was reduced to care and maintenance and the garrison withdrawn. Dunree Fort was to continue as an operational coast defence fort for a few more years but the last full-charge practice firing of the guns took place on 27 April

1949. In 1952 the decision was taken to disband the Coast Defence Artillery and the guns at Dunree were placed in a state of 'long maintenance'. Two Master Gunners, one responsible for the guns at Lenan and the other for the guns at Dunree, and a small cadre were retained at Dunree as maintenance staff. They were administered by the 4th Artillery Regiment stationed at Mullingar.[1]

Although Fort Dunree's days as a coastal defence fortification were over, it continued to be used for training purposes by the Forsa Cosanta Aitiuil (FCA), the volunteer reserve force which supported the Irish regular army. The guns did, however, fire once more in the summer of 1964 when one gun was fired by a detachment from the Southern Command FCA Coast Defence. Finally, in 1968, the guns were partly dismantled so that they could no longer be fired but they remained in position.[2]

There was a final brief spurt of activity at the fort in August 1969 when troops of the 14th Infantry Group prepared the camp as a centre for refugees. Severe sectarian rioting had broken out in Northern Ireland at that time and many Catholic families were fleeing their homes. In the event the fort was not used and this was the last occasion on which regular troops of the Irish army were garrisoned there though it did continue to be used as a training camp by the FCA until 1983.[3]

The defences today

Despite the passage of over 50 years, all of the forts and batteries on Lough Swilly can still be seen today though their condition varies greatly. In 1986 the old fort at Dunree was officially opened as a military museum with exhibits showing the history of the fort. The battery, with two 6-inch (152-mm) BL guns still in place, is not yet part of the museum though it is possible to walk up the hill to see the guns but the magazines and crew shelter beneath are derelict. Above the battery the redoubt also remains intact but the guardroom and storeroom inside are also derelict. The camp below the battery is in reasonable condition though the corrugated iron huts are beginning to deteriorate and there is an urgent need to find alternate uses for the accommodation.

Ned's Point Fort at Buncrana was painstakingly refurbished by Buncrana Borough Council in the early 1990s only to be completely vandalised almost immediately after the work was completed. The fort is now closed to the public. Lenan camp has also been

demolished and all the corrugated iron accommodation huts dating from World War One have been levelled. Only the brick-built married quarters, the guard house and the gaunt brick chimneys of the vanished buildings still

The old fort at Dunree which is now a military museum.

Author

Today Lenan Fort lies derelict and vandalised.   *Author*

stand. However, the gun pits of the battery are in reasonable condition including the smaller central pit which was originally built to hold a single 9.2-inch (233-mm) BL Mk I gun. The magazines, shell rooms, cartridge stores and connecting corridors can still be visited and the remains of the cartridge and shell hoists are still in place. Sadly, much of the battery area has been used as a rubbish tip for a number of years.

The fourth fort on the eastern shore, Inch Fort, is privately owned and is also derelict. The barrack block to the rear of the fort has been converted into a private house but the concrete gun pits, rear wall and small caponier remain. There is also a more modern single-storey building inside the fort but this is in poor condition. The approach to the fort is by means of a private road that passes the house.

On the western shore of the lough the forts which were not modernised at the end of the nineteenth century are in better condition and all are being used. The fort at Rathmullen has now been converted into the local heritage centre and is open to the public The defensible guard house is well maintained and it is worth asking to visit the gun platform where the pivots for the two guns can still be seen. The other two forts, Macamish and Knockalla, are now holiday homes and are not open to visitors. Both are in excellent condition and their current use does at least mean that the structures are maintained and kept watertight.

Greencastle Fort on Lough Foyle has been used as a hotel for many years and so it too is in good condition. The most recent owner has taken a keen interest in the

fort's history and has renovated and converted the buildings sympathetically. The integrity of the fort has been retained and until recently the fort has been open to the public. Now, however, the hotel has been put up for sale and its future appears uncertain. Across the lough the Martello tower at Magilligan Point is also in good condition, having been refurbished by the Northern Ireland Department of the Environment Heritage Service which has removed World War Two accretions. Further work is continuing on the tower with a view to eventually opening it to the public, but at the moment it can only be viewed from the outside.

Most of the other World War Two structures at Magilligan Point have now gone, thanks either to the ravages of the sea or the local council. By the early 1950s the searchlight positions for the emergency battery had collapsed into the sea due to erosion, and a number of pillboxes were demolished by Limavady District Council when Magilligan beach was developed as a leisure facility and nature reserve. A few remnants of the emergency battery can still be found hidden in the sand hills behind the Point Bar. In the sand dunes above the public house there is still a concrete platform for a 6-inch (152-mm) BL gun with ready-use lockers built into the sides of the platform. There is also a sunken brick magazine and the concrete platform and holdfast for the 12-pdr QF gun.

Only a few of the many pillboxes built to defend Magilligan beach are still there and one of these is the two-storey pillbox at Magilligan Point on the shore opposite the public house. There is also a more traditional

The left hand gun position at Orlock has been converted into a private house.   *Author*

pillbox halfway along Magilligan beach up against the sand dunes and in the middle of the danger area of the Ministry of Defence firing range. A third pillbox, constructed of black basalt, can still be found near the car park at Downhill and there is another, this time made of brick, in the middle of a field defending a minor road over Binevenagh Mountain. The pillboxes at the northern end of the Bann Line at the Barmouth have been destroyed but others remain on Tyrella beach near Newcastle in County Down and around a number of the airfields used during World War Two.

On Belfast Lough, Carrickfergus Castle is a scheduled historic monument and open to the public. Although the displays tend to concentrate on the castle's earlier Norman history, it still retains a number of 32-pdr SB guns on the Grand Battery and four 80-pdr RML 5-ton guns on their original traversing platforms. Grey Point Fort at Helen's Bay has been completely refurbished by the Grey Point Fort Committee in conjunction with the Department of the Environment Heritage Service and is open to the public. Although the original guns of the fort had been scrapped after the disbandment of the coast artillery in 1956, the Committee managed to obtain two guns from the Irish Department of Defence. Both guns are 6-inch (152-mm) BL Mk VIIs and came from the defences of Cork harbour – one from Spike Island and the other from Fort Davis (or Fort Carlisle as it was called prior to 1922). The refurbished fort was formally opened in 1986 and today is one of the best preserved coast defence batteries in the United Kingdom.

Of the other batteries around Belfast Lough and Larne nothing now remains except at Orlock Point. The battery sites at Kilroot and Larne have now been completely built over with a salt works at Kilroot and a leisure centre at

Larne. At Orlock, however, both gun houses can still be seen though each has now been converted into a private house, one with an upper storey added to it. The two searchlight positions are also still there but both are derelict and in danger of destruction by the sea.

During World War Two more than twenty HAA battery sites were built throughout Northern Ireland but today little can be seen of these sites. Four HAA sites can still be found reasonably easily: LO7 at Magilligan Point, which is now inside the Ministry of Defence training area; LR3 on farmland overlooking Brown's Bay at Islandmagee near Larne; U8 on farmland near Comber in County Down; and BA2 at Ballymacormick Point between Bangor and Groomsport, also in County Down. Ballymacormick Point is now owned by the National Trust but access is permitted though the remaining gun pits are really only visible in the winter since in the summer they are heavily overgrown by gorse bushes.

So, in fact, Northern Ireland and County Donegal are fortunate that the majority of the permanent sites constructed for their defence between 1796 and 1956 still exist. However, fewer of World War Two sites remain since these were, by their very nature, less substantial, built in a hurry, occupied for only a short time, and frequently sited on commercially valuable real estate. At Dunree, Rathmullen, Grey Point, Carrickfergus and Magilligan Point steps have been taken to preserve the forts for posterity as a reminder of Ulster's turbulent past. It is now important that every effort should be made to ensure the preservation of Macamish Martello Tower, Knockalla Fort and Greencastle Fort which are still in relatively good condition and to repair the depredations of the vandals at Ned's Point Fort. The battery and redoubt at Dunree are in urgent need of preservation, particularly as the guns are still in place in the battery, but there seems to be little hope for Inch Fort unless an acceptable use can be found for it.

It is important that some of the modern structures should also be preserved as a memorial to the sacrifices made by the people of Northern Ireland during World War Two, and for the instruction of future generations. However, modern concrete does not have the attraction of granite worked by craftsmen for today's visitors and, sadly, it is likely that these structures will be allowed to crumble away. Let us hope that some will survive and that the current attempts to survey and photograph those sites presently remaining will at least provide an effective record for the future – an aim which it is hoped this book will help to achieve.

APPENDIX A

Artillery guns and mortars in use or proposed for the defences of Ulster between 1796 and 1956

Smooth-bore

Type	Weight (cwt)	Length (feet)	Calibre (inches)	Range (yards)	Comments
9-pdr	26.00	7.50	4.20	1600	
12-pdr	29.00	7.50	4.62	1650	
	42.00	9.00	4.62	1700	
18-pdr	42.00	9.00	5.29	1780	
24-pdr	50.00	9.50	5.82	1850	
42-pdr	84.00	10.00	7.00	2250	English gun*
56-pdr	97.00	11.00	7.56	2100	
68-pdr	112.00	10.80	8.12	2200	

* The dimensions and performance of the French gun are assumed to be similar though the range might not have been as great.

Type	Weight (cwt)	Length (feet)	Calibre (inches)	Range (yards)	Comments
Shell Gun 8 in	65.00	9.00	8.05	1920	
Carronade 24-pdr	13.00	3.75	5.68	1150	
Howitzer 5.5 in (iron)	9.50	2.67	5.66	1700	Range at 12 degrees
8-in Brass	12.75	3.08	8.00	1700	Range at 12 degrees
Mortar 13-in Land Service	37.25	3.67	13.00	690 – 2900	Range at 45 degrees with varying charges. Wt of shell 200 lbs.

Rifled muzzle-loading guns

Type	Weight (cwt)	Length (feet)	Calibre (inches)	Range (yards)	Comments
64-pdr	64.00	9.50	6.39	4000	
	71.00	10.22	6.29	3500	Converted 8 in SB
80-pdr	5 tons	11.37	6.29	3750	Converted 68-pdr SB
9 in	12 tons	13.00	9.00	4000	Wt of shell 256 lbs

Rifled breech-loading guns

Type	Weight (cwt)	Length (feet)	Calibre (inches)	Range (yards)	Comments
7 in	82.00	10.00	7.00	3500	Wt of shell 110 lbs

Breech-loading guns

Type	Weight (cwt)	Length (feet)	Calibre (inches)	Range (yards)	Comments
5-in Mk II	38.00	11.75	5.00	5000	
6-in Mk VI	5.00 tons	14.50	6.00	8000	
6-in Mk VII	7.53 tons	23.26	6.00	12000	
9.2-in Mk I	22.00 tons	21.25	9.20	10000	
9.2-in Mk IV	23.00 tons	25.85	9.20	16000	
9.2-in Mk X	28.00 tons	36.86	9.20	17500	Eventually increased to 29000 yards

Quick-firing guns

Type	Weight (cwt)	Length (feet)	Calibre (inches)	Range (yards)	Comments
3-pdr Mk I	4.00	6.75	1.85	5000	Hotchkiss
6-pdr Mk I	8.00	8.10	2.25	5500	Hotchkiss
6-pdr Twin	10.00	12.00	2.25	5500	
12-pdr	12.00	10.25	3.00	9000	
4.7-in Mk IV	42.00	16.17	4.70	11800	

Anti-aircraft guns

Type	Weight (cwt)	Length (feet)	Calibre (inches)	Range (yards)	Comments
40-mm LAA	2.05 tons[1]	13.00	1.57	5000 feet[2]	Mobile Eqpt
3-in HAA	5.94 tons[1]	11.60	3.00	23500 feet[2]	Mobile Eqpt
3.7-in HAA	9.15 tons[1]	20.00	3.70	32000 feet[2]	Mobile Eqpt

[1] Complete weight of equipment.
[2] Maximum effective ceiling

APPENDIX B

FIRE CONTROL EQUIPMENT

With the old smooth-bore guns, fire control in the forts and batteries around the coast was essentially the responsibility of each gun captain rather as it was on board the old wooden men-of-war. However, the increased range of the new rifled guns required a more sophisticated form of control. Initially guns were controlled by an officer in an observation post who was able to observe the fall of shot and who passed corrections to the guns by various methods including speaking tube, megaphone or mechanical indicator.

This simple form of fire control was still essentially inaccurate since it relied upon the officer in the observation post accurately estimating the range to the target by eye. There was an urgent need for a device that could accurately estimate the range to the target and between 1870 and 1880 a number of range finding devices were tried out. Most required two observers spaced widely apart using instruments to measure the two base angles of the triangle which was formed. This system required a piece of flat ground up to 440 yards (400 metres) wide and it was often very difficult to find a suitable piece of ground in close proximity to many of the coastal forts.

It was Captain HSS Watkin RA who produced a practical solution to the problem when in the 1880s he realised that if the observer was above the waterline this height became the base of the measuring triangle. So a measurement of the angle of depression to the bow-waterline of the target automatically gave the range. The Watkin depression rangefinder became the standard range-finding equipment in every fort and battery along the coast with the information it provided being relayed to the guns by means of an electric telegraph.

A further problem facing the gunners was the fact that the target ship was moving and a method had to be devised to compute the amount the gun should be 'laid-off' to ensure that the shell would hit the target. Once again Captain Watkin came up with an answer by developing the Depression Position Finder. This equipment comprised a telescopic sight linked to a plotting table and an electrical transmission system. The position finder was installed in a protected concrete bunker known as a 'cell' which was sited some distance from the guns and manned by trained observers. One of these observers kept the sight trained on the target while the other used the plotter to predict the time of flight of the shell. With the position finder it was not necessary for the officer on the gun position to make a correction for displacement, but using the depression rangefinder a displacement scale was needed and the officer had continually to correct the ranges given on the dials.

Perhaps the greatest advantage of the position finder over the basic rangefinder was that the former did not have to be placed close to the guns while the latter did. Indeed, using the position finder to lay the guns meant that targets could be engaged which were actually invisible to the guns and the observer at the position finder cell could fire the guns, if necessary. By the turn of the century the Watkin position finders and rangefinders were being installed in coast defence forts and batteries throughout the United Kingdom and overseas throughout the dominions and colonies. Position finders were provided for batteries armed with heavy 9.2-inch (233-mm) BL guns and the depression rangefinder for batteries mounting 6-inch (152-mm) BL guns and in practice batteries.

During World War Two the numerous emergency batteries installed for the defence of ports and beaches initially did not have position finders or depression rangefinders and, instead, were provided with Barr and Stroud optical rangefinders. The model supplied for the three batteries in Northern Ireland was the 12-foot (3.17-metre) rangefinder. This equipment consisted of two telescopes mounted in a common frame with a common eyepiece in the middle of the frame. When measuring the range, the rangefinder itself formed the base of a triangle having at its apex the object, the range of which was determined by measuring the parallax. Invented in 1882, the Barr and Stroud rangefinder used the 'coincidence' system to obtain the range to the target. In this system the field of view is divided into two parts by a fine dividing line and the range to the object is obtained by bringing the image of the object on one side of the dividing line into exact coincidence with the corresponding image on the other side.

The position finders, depression rangefinders and the Barr and Stroud rangefinders were best suited for use when engaging relatively slow moving targets at medium to long range. However, the advent of fast moving torpedo boats and destroyers produced the problem that there was very little time for the guns to range because of the speed of the target. This was particularly the case at night when attempting to engage a target as it crossed the narrow area of water illuminated by a dispersed beam searchlight. The solution to the problem was the development of the auto-sight. This sight, when laid on the bow-waterline of the target, automatically gave the gun the necessary elevation for the range and was fitted to all guns which were likely to be used to engage fast targets at short range, particularly at night. Naval guns which, in 1940, were provided for the emergency batteries were not equipped with the auto-sight.

Where batteries were only equipped with rangefinders there was a need to provide the guns with details of the bearing to the target. Major AH Dumaresq RE provided the answer by developing a method of measuring the bearing to the target using a circular plate marked in degrees from 1 to 360. In the centre of the plate there was a pivoted arm with an eyehole and a V-shaped sight. To obtain the bearing, the plate was oriented on North and the V sight laid on the target.

A further wartime improvement to the fire control system for the guns at Grey Point and Kilroot was the introduction of MAGSLIP. This permitted the automatic electrical transmission of bearing and range from the BOP to the guns. Finally, in 1954, a mobile radar was installed in each of the forts. This was the Equipment Radar AA No 3 Mk 2/7 which was used to provide both range and bearing to the target for the guns.

NOTES

Abbreviations

MA   Military Archives, Dublin
NAM   National Army Museum, London
NLI   National Library of Ireland
PRO   Public Record Office, London
TCD   Trinity College Library, Dublin

Introduction

1. RG Morton, 'Plans for Ulster Defence 1795–97', *The Irish Sword*, Vol II, No 8
2. JH Rose, *Life of Napoleon*, Vol I, Bell & Sons, London, 1929, p 170

1 THE BOARD OF ORDNANCE AND THE DEFENCE COMMITTEES

1. PRO WO 55/833
2. Ibid
3. PRO WO 55/835
4. Ibid

2 WAR WITH FRANCE, 1798–1809

1. PRO HO 100/67
2. NLI Kilmainham Papers, Ms 1116 f232
3. NLI Ms 175, f494
4. TCD Ms 942, Vol II, f190
5. PRO WO 55/831
6. PRO WO 73
7. Ibid
8. PRO WO 55/831
9. Ibid
10. Ibid
11. NLI Ms 15 b 1 (19)
12. NLI Ms 175, f491
13. PRO WO 55/831
14. NLI Kilmainham Papers, Ms 1132, f232
15. PRO WO 44/110

3 LOUGH SWILLY, 1810–1815

1. PRO WO 55/832; PRO WO 55/833
2. PRO WO 55/833
3. Ibid
4. Ibid
5. Ibid
6. Ibid
7. Rose, Napoleon, Vol II, p 229

8. PRO WO 55/833
9. Ordnance Survey of Ireland, *Memoirs of Ireland, Vol 38, Parishes of Co Donegal 1 1833–1835*, Institute of Irish Studies, Queen's University of Belfast, Belfast, 1997, p 25
10. PRO WO 55/836
11. TCD Ms 942, Vol II, f190
12. PRO MPH 1/765
13. PRO WO 55/836
14. PRO WO 55/2477
15. PRO WO 44/109

4 LOUGH FOYLE AND BELFAST LOUGH, 1810–1816

1. PRO WO 55/832
2. PRO WO 55/833
3. PRO WO 55/835
4. Ibid
5. Ibid
6. Col George RE Lewis, 'Report on the Application of Forts, Towers and Batteries to Coast Defences and Harbours', *Professional Papers of the Royal Engineers*, Vol VII, 1844
7. PRO WO 55/833
8. Ordnance Survey of Ireland, *Memoirs of Ireland, Vol 11, Parishes of Co Londonderry III, 1831–1835*, Institute of Irish Studies, Queen's University of Belfast, Belfast, 1991, p 85
9. PRO WO 55/834
10. PRO WO 46/27
11. PRO WO 55/835

5 THE IRISH SIGNAL TOWERS

1. PRO HO 100/120, f.2977
2. NLI Kilmainham Papers, Ms 119, ff 368–9
3. Ibid
4. Ibid
5. Ibid
6. Quoted in Paul M Kerrigan, *Castles and Fortifications in Ireland 1495–1945*, The Collins Press, Cork, 1995, p 160
7. PRO HO 100/121, ff 130–4; PRO HO 100/127, ff 90–2; PRO HO 100–33, ff 25/25; also Kerrigan op cit pp 276–80

6 THE YEARS OF PEACE, 1816–1854

1. PRO WO 44/109
2. PRO WO 55/1750
3. PRO WO 55/843

4. PRO WO 55/850
5. PRO WO 55/846
6. PRO WO 55/849
7. PRO WO 55/846
8. PRO WO 55/851

7 FEAR OF FRANCE AND THE TECHNOLOGICAL REVOLUTION, 1855–1880

1. Quoted in Norman Longmate, *Island Fortress*, Grafton, London, 1993, pp 321–2
2. PRO WO 55/847
3. PRO WO 33/5
4. Ibid
5. PRO WO 396/1
6. Ibid
7. NAM The Papers of Gen Sir James Warre
8. PRO WO 35/40
9. PRO WO 396/1

8 BREECH-LOADERS AND BATTLESHIPS, 1881–1900

1. PRO WO 33/39
2. Ibid
3. PRO WO 396/1
4. Ibid
5. Ibid
6. Ibid
7. Ibid
8. Ibid
9. PRO WO 32/6376
10. PRO WO 396/4
11. PRO WO 396/5
12. Ibid

9 THE APPROACH OF WAR, 1900–1914

1. PRO WO 78/4915
2. PRO MPHH 1/326
3. PRO WO 33/323
4. PRO CAB 16/1
5. Ibid
6. PRO WO 33/401
7. MA Lenan Fort Book

10 WORLD WAR ONE, 1914–1918

1. PRO WO 33/2859
2. PRO WO 78/4419
3. Ibid
4. *Official History of World War I, Naval Operations, Vol II*, pp 392–6
5. Ibid
6. PRO WO 78/4873 and PRO WO 33/944
7. *Official History of World War I, Naval Operations Vol II*, p 338
8. PRO WO 95/5456 and 5457

11 BETWEEN THE WARS, 1919–1939

1. PRO CAB 36/16
2. PRO CAB 53/36
3. PRO CAB 13/2
4. PRO CAB 13/4
5. Ibid
6. Ibid
7. PRO CAB 3/6

12 WORLD WAR TWO – PART ONE, 1939–1941

1. PRO WO 166/1727
2. Ibid
3. Ibid
4. Ibid
5. PRO WO 166/1179
6. PRO WO 166/1727
7. Ibid
8. Ibid
9. PRO WO 166/271 and PRO WO 166/744
10. PRO WO 166/655
11. PRO CAB 3/8
12. *The Official History of the Second World War, The Defence of the United Kingdom*, Basil Collier, HMSO, London, 1957, pp 504–6

13 WORLD WAR TWO – PART TWO, 1942–1945

1. PRO WO 166/6681
2. PRO WO 199/2932
3. PRO WO 166/7374
4. John W Blake, *Northern Ireland in the Second World War*, HMSO, London, 1956, pp 360 and 364
5. Ibid, p 183
6. 'The Emergency', *The Irish Sword*, Vol XIX, Nos 75 and 76, p 97
7. PRO WO 166/271
8. John P Duggan, *A History of the Irish Army*, Gill and MacMillan, Dublin, 1991, p 208

Epilogue

1. Commandant Declan O'Carroll, *The Guns of Dunree*, Fort Dunree Military Museum, 1986, pp 12–13
2. Ibid
3. Ibid

BIBLIOGRAPHY

Articles

Campbell, Jack, 'Coastal Defences of Lenan', *Donegal Annual 1991*

Doherty, Richard, '3rd (Ulster) Anti-Aircraft Brigade, RA, (SR)', *The Irish Sword*, Vol XVIII, No 71, Summer 1991

Emerson, Lieutenant Lucius J, 'The Swilly Forts', *An Cosantoir*, Vol XII, No 6, June 1962

Fitzgerald, John, 'The Heather Fort', *Donegal Annual 1979*

Keogh, Dermot, and Dolan, Aengus, 'Anglo-Irish Diplomatic Relations and World War II', *The Irish Sword*, Vol XIX, Nos 75 and 76, 1993–1994

Kerrigan, Paul M, 'The French Expedition to Bantry Bay, 1796', *The Irish Sword*, Vol XXI, No 83, Summer 1998

Kinsella, Anthony, 'The Pettigo-Belleek Triangle Incident', *The Irish Sword*, Vol XX, No 82, No 36, Summer 1970

Macauley, JA, 'General Dumouriez and Irish Defence', *The Irish Sword*, Vol IX, Nos 35 and 36, Winter 1969 and Summer 1970

McKay, Russell, 'The Fortifications of Lough Swilly and Lough Foyle: Temporary Expedients 1798–1800', *Donegal Annual 1977*

Stevenson, Ian V, 'Two Treaty Ports and One That Never Was', *Fortress*, Nos 12 and 13, 1992

Van Brock, FW, 'A Memoir of 1798', *The Irish Sword*, Vol IX, No 36, Summer 1970

Books

Blake, John W, *Northern Ireland in the Second World War*, HMSO, London, 1965

Brown, Ian and Burridge, David, *Twentieth Century Defences in Britain, An Introductory Guide*, Council for British Archaeology, York, 1995

Collier, Basil, *History of the Second World War, The Defence of the United Kingdom*, HMSO, London, 1957

Duggan, John P, *A History of the Irish Army*, Gill and Macmillan, Dublin, 1991

Fisk, Robert, *In Time of War*, Andre Deutsch Ltd, London, 1983

Hezlet, Sir Arthur, *The 'B' Specials*, The Mourne River Press, Belfast, 1997

Hogg, Ian V, *Allied Artillery of World War One*, Crowood Press, Marlborough, London, 1998

— *Coast Defences of England and Wales 1856–1956*, David & Charles, Newton Abbott, 1974

Hughes, Major General BP, *British Smooth-Bore Artillery*, Arms and Armour Press, London, 1969

Jellicoe, Admiral Earl, *The Grand Fleet 1914–1916*, Cassell & Co, London, 1919

— *The Submarine Peril*, Cassell & Co, London, 1934

Kee, Robert, *The Green Flag*, Weidenfeld and Nicolson, London, 1972

Kerrigan, Paul M, *Castles and Fortifications in Ireland 1485–1945*, The Collins Press, Cork, 1995

Longmate, Norman, *Island Fortress*, Grafton, London, 1993

Maurice-Jones, Colonel KW, *The History of the Coast Artillery in the British Army*, RA Institution, London, 1959

Newbolt, Henry, *Official History of World War One, Naval Operations*, Vols I and V, Longmans Green and Co, London, 1931

O'Carroll, Commandant Declan, *The Guns of Dunree*, Dunree Military Museum, 1987

Ordnance Survey of Ireland, *Memoirs of Ireland, Vol 11, Parishes of Co Londonderry III, 1831–1835*, Institute of Irish Studies, Queen's University of Belfast, Belfast, 1991

— *Memoirs of Ireland, Vol 37, Parishes of Co Antrim XIV, 1832, 1839–1840*, Institute of Irish Studies, Queen's University of Belfast, Belfast, 1996

— *Memoirs of Ireland, Vol 38, Parishes of Co Donegal I, 1833–1835*, Institute of Irish Studies, Queen's University of Belfast, Belfast, 1997

Padfield, Peter, *The Battleship Era*, Rupert Hart-Davis Ltd, London, 1972

Rose, JH, *Life of Napoleon*, Bell and Sons, London, 1929

Saunders, Andrew, *Fortress Britain*, Beaufort, Liphook, 1989

INDEX

Italics indicate a picture of, or relating to, the subject.

Amiens, Peace of   22
Antrim Artillery Militia   43, 65, 68
Antrim Royal Garrison Artillery (SR)   57, *57*, 68, 69, 75, 78
Armada   11
Armstrong, Sir William   47-48, *48*, 54-55

Ballina   14
Ballinamuck   14, 15
Ballymacormick Point   97, 99, 106
Ballyshannon   7, 8-9, 24-25, 43
Bangor   69, 90, 93, 95, 97, 99, 106
Bantry Bay   12-13, 15, 20, 22, 40, 42, 76
Bateman, John   27
Belfast   7, *9*, 11, 12, 23-24, 37, 39, 42, 49, 51, 55, 56, 57, 58, 63, 64, 65, 66, 67, 68, 69, 73-75, 77, 78, 80, 81, 82, 83, 86, 92, 93, 94, 95, 98, 99, 102, 103
Belfast District Defence Scheme   63, 83
Belfast Lough   7, 8, 11, 12, 20, 23-24, 26, 37, 39, 43, 49, 51, 52, 55, 56, 57, 61, 65, 69, 74-75, 80, 83, 85, 90, 93, 96, 97, 98, 106
Belfast Lough Fixed Defences   86, 87, 88
Belleek   (see Forts – Belleek)
Bentra   75
Bere Island   12, 13, 20, 76
Berehaven   57, 64, 76, 78, 101
Berlin, SMS   71
Blakely, Capt Alexander   47
Bompard, Commodore   14, 15, 20
British Army   17, 47, 77, 80, 88, *92*, 96, 100, 102
  Corps
  III Corps   92, 96, 98
  VI Corps   89, 90, 91, 92
  Divisions
  5th Infantry   92, 96, 99
  45th Infantry   98, 99
  53rd (Welsh) Infantry   91, 92
  59th Infantry   96, 98
  61st Infantry   90, 91, 96, 98

Brigades
3rd (Ulster) AA (SR)   84, 85, 92, 93, 95, 96
17th Infantry   77, 101
Lancashire & Cheshire Heavy Bde RA   81, 83
Armour
North Irish Horse (SR)   84, 90
Artillery
Antrim Heavy Regt RA (TA)   87, 89
429th (Antrim) Coast Regt RA (TA)   103, *104*
525th (Antrim) Coast Regiment RA   89, 90, 98, 99, 103
1st HAA Regt RA   95, *97*
8th (Belfast) HAA Regt RA (SR)   84, 92
9th (Londonderry) HAA Regt RA (SR)   84, 92
102nd HAA Regt RA   92, 93
111th HAA Regt RA   95
126th HAA Regt RA   97
141st HAA Regt RA   99
188th (M) HAA Regt RA   99
66th LAA Regt RA   93
144th LAA Regt RA   99
3rd (Ulster) Searchlight Regt RA (SR)   84
15th Company RGA   63, 65, 68, 69, 75
113th Coast Bty RA   90
114th Coast Bty RA   90
115th Coast Bty RA   90
380th Coast Bty RA   89, 90
381st Coast Bty RA   90
17th Heavy Bty RA   78, 80
188th (Antrim) Heavy Bty RA (TA)   *82*, 83, 86, 87, 89, 103
200th Heavy Bty RA   87, 89
309th HAA Bty RA   92
315th HAA Bty RA   93
431st HAA Bty RA   93
434th (Independent) HAA Bty RA   99
146th (Z) Bty RA   93
Engineers
74th (Antrim Artillery) Engineer Regt RE (Volunteers)   *82*, 103
146th Field Engineer Regt RE (TA)   103
33rd Fortress Company RE   69
Antrim Fortress Company RE (TA)   *82*, 83, 89

Renfrew Fortress Company RE (TA) 81

Infantry

3rd Bn Royal Inniskilling Fusiliers (SR) 69, 73

4th Bn Royal Inniskilling Fusiliers 69, 73

5th Bn Royal Inniskilling Fusiliers (SR) 90

3rd Bn Royal Irish Fusiliers (SR) 69, 72-73

5th Bn Royal Irish Fusliers (SR) 91

3rd Bn Royal Irish Rifles (SR) 69

4th Bn Royal Irish Rifles (SR) 69

5th Bn Royal Irish Rifles (SR) 69

6th Bn Royal Ulster Rifles 90

7th Bn Royal Ulster Rifles 91

Miscellaneous

7th Anti-Aircraft Group 96, 99

British Troops Northern Ireland (BTNI) 92, 96, 98

34th (Antrim) Fire Command 75

35th (Donegal) Fire Command 75

18th Military Mission 96

Brown's Bay 106

Buncrana 18, *18*, 21, 22, *22*, 27, 30, 32, 34, 42, 44, 52, 55, 58, 61, *61*, 73, 77, 78, 101, 104

Calder, Rear Adm Sir Robert, RN 40

Cardew, Capt George, RE 27, 34, 35

Campbell, Messrs & Son 63, 67

Carhampton, Lord 13, 20

Carlingford Lough 7, 49

Carrickfergus 7, *9*, 11, 23, 37, 51, 55, 56, 65, 75, 83, 103, 106

Carrickfergus Castle 8, *9*, 11, 23, *24*, 37, *38*, 42, 43, *44*, 49, *49*, 51, *51*, 52, 57, *57*, 63, 68, 69, 81, 90, 106

Carrigan Head 40, *40*, 41

Cavan, Earl of 20

Chappe, Claud 39

Charlemont 25

Coast Brigade, RA 52, 103

Colhoun, Robert 63

Committees

Defence 19, 52, 56, 57, 58, 78, 81, 82

Esher 19

Heavy Gun 19

Home Ports Defence 19, 81, 82

Imperial Defence 19

Joint Naval and Military 19, 57

Joint Overseas and Home Defence 19, 78

Morley 55

Owen 64, 65, 79

RA & RE Works 19, 56, 57, 58, 60, 61, 63

Committee of Engineers 17, 18, 23, 26, 30, 34

Cork 17, 40, 41, 42, 49, 50, 64, 76, 78, 85, *100*, 101, 102, 104, 106

Cork Artillery Militia 68

Cork Royal Garrison Artillery (SR) 78

Cotton, Lt Col BD, RA (TA) 102

D'Arcy, Lt Col Robert, RE 23, 26

de Valera, Eamon 79, 89, 96, 99

Doe Castle 20, *20*

Donegal 7, 14, 15, 20, 24, 26, 28, *29*, 34, *35*, 40, *40*, 41, 76, 77, 78, 100, 101, 102, 106

Donegal Artillery Militia 43, 63

Dumouriez, Gen François 26

Dunaff Head 7, 59, 72, 80

East Twin Island 68, 73, *74*, 80, 93

Easter Rebellion 76

Ebrington Barracks 43, 89

Edgar, Mr 18, 27, 30, 34

Edgeworth, Richard Lovell 39

Edgeworthstown Yeomanry 39

Elswick Ordnance Company 55

Emmet, Robert 22

Enniskillen 7, 24, 25, 43, 52, 77

Examination Service 69, 81, 86, 99, 101

Fahan 21, 23, 27, 77, 78

Fanad Head 7, 21, 41, 58, 64, 69

Farrell, Edward 34-35

Fisher, Col Benjamin, RE 17, 18, 22, 26, 27, 31, 34

Fitzgerald, Lord Edward 13

Forsa Cosanta Aitiuil (FCA) 104

Forts

Belleek 25, *25*, 43, 77, *79*

Camden 50, 101

Carlisle 50, 106

Down of Inch (Inch) 21, 22, 26, 32-33, *32*, 42, 43, *54*, 55, 59, 61, *61*, 63, 65, 77, 78, 105, 106

Dunree (East) 21, 22, 23, 26, 27, 28, *29*, 30, 42, 43, 44, 58, 59, *59*, 60, 61, 64, 65, 67, 68, 69, 71, *71*, 72, *72*, 73, 75, 76, 78, 79, 80, *80*, *81*, 100, 101, 102, *102*, 104, *104*, 106

Greencastle 7, 26, 34, 35, *35*, 36, *36*, 37, 42, 43, *50*, 51, 52, 55, 56, 58, *58*, 78, 105, 106

Grey Point 49, 51, 55, 56, 57, 61, *66*, 67, 68, 69, 73, 74, 81, *82*, 83, *83*, 86, 87, *87*, 88, *88*, 89, 90, 97, 98, 99, 103, 106, 110

Kilroot 56, 61, 67, *67*, 68, 69, 73, 74, 81, 83, 86, 87, 89, 90, 102, 103, 106, 110

Knockalla (West) 21, *21*, 22, 23, 26, 27, 28, 30, *30*, 33, 36, 42, 43, 52, 56, 64, 105, 106

Lenan 58, 59, 60, 62, *62*, 64, 65, *65*, 68, 69, 71, 72, *72*, 74, 75, 76, 78, 79, 80, 100, *100*, 101, 102, 104, *105*

Ned's Point 21, 22, 23, 26, 27, 30, 31, 32, 33, 42, *48*, 52, *54*, 55, 56, 58, 59, *60*, 61, *61*, 63, *63*, 65, 70, 104, 106

Rathmullen 7, 8, 21, 22, 23, 26, 30, 32, *32*, 33, 42, 43, 52, 61, 73, 101, 105, 106

French Ships

Anacreon 14

Fraternite 12

Hoche 15, *15*, 20, 21, 22, 28, 56

La Gloire 45

Seduisant 12

Gladstone, Mr 50

Graham, Lt Col OB, RA 87, 97, 99

Grand Fleet, The 69, 70, 71

Grey Point (see Forts – Grey Point)

Hardwick, Lord 39, 40

Hardy, Gen 14, 15

Harland & Wolff 94, 95

Harte, Capt John 20

Harvey, Maj Charles Bateson 61

Helen's Bay 51, 88, 106

Hill, Sir George 20, 34

Holywood 49, 51, 55, 86, 93

Humbert, Gen 14, 15

Inch 7, 21, 22, 26, 32-33, 42

Inishowen Peninsula 7, 77, 79, 100, 102

Inspector General of Fortifications 17, 18, 19, 22, 23, 27, 28, 34, 43

Invalid Detachment, RA 42, 52

Irish Army 80, *81*, 96, *100*, *102*, 104

4th Artillery Regt 104

5th Coast Bty 80, 100, 101

6th Coast Bty 80, 100

Engineers Coast Defence Company 101

17th Infantry Bn 101

Killala 14

Knox, Thomas 20, 34

Lake, General 13, 14

Lancaster, CW 47

Lancey, Lt W, RE 8, 28

Larne 49, 69, 75, 89, 90, 95, 98, 99, 103, 106

Lenan Head (see Forts – Lenan)

Lewis, Col George, RE 36, 47

Londonderry 7, 8, 11, 20, 26, 34, 39, 42, 43, 49, 58, 63, 65, 69, 73, 76, 77, 78, 80, *84*, 89, 93, 94, 95, 96, 97, 99

Londonderry Defence Scheme 65

Lough Erne 7, 24, 52, 77, 95, 98

Lough Foyle 7, 8, 17, 20, 23, 26, 34, 42, 44, 49, 51, 52, 55, 56, 57, 58, 73, 85, 89, 92, 96, 105

Lough Neagh 25, 91

Lough Swilly 7, 8, 15, *15*, 17, 18, 20, 21, 22, *22*, 23, 26, 27, 28, 30, 32, 33, 34, 35, 37, 41, 42, 43, *48*, 51, 52, 55, 56, 57, 58, 59, 61, 63, 64, 65, 68, 69, 70, *70*, 71, *71*, 72, 73, 75, 76, 77, 78, 80, 85, 91, 96, 99, 100, 101, 102, 103, 104

Lough Swilly Fortress 64

Macamish Point 21, 22, 26, 30, 37, 70

Magilligan Martello Tower 36, *36*, 37, *37*, 56, 78, 89, 90, 105

Magilligan Point 7, 20, 26, 34, 35, 36, *36*, 37, 56, 78, 89, *89*, 90, 91, *91*, 92, *93*, 99, 103, 105, 106

Malin 101, 102

Malin Head 39, 40, *40*, 41, *41*

Mann, Brig Gen Gother, RE 18, 23, 31, 34, 36

Melmore Head 41

Milford Haven 50, 54, 56, 98

Moncreiff, Capt 54, 55
Morse, Lt Gen 22, 27
Mountjoy, Lord 11
Mulroy Bay 64
Musgrave Channel 68

Napoleon III 45, 47, 49
National Defence Corps 86, 87, 91
Newry 7, 49
North Channel 12, 58, 74, 75
Northern Ireland Fixed Defences 90

O'Neill, Hugh 11, 25, 32
Ordnance, Board of 8, 17, 18, 19, 24, 26, 27, 34, 35, 38, 39,
    42, 43, 45, 47
Ordnance, Master Gen of 17, 18, 45
Orlock Point 68, 69, 84, 86, 90, 97, 98, 103, 106, *106*

Paixhans, Gen 45, 47
Palace Barracks 86
Paris, Treaty of 49
Plan 'W' 91, 96, *97*
Power, First Lt Robert, RE 27

Rathmullen (see Forts – Rathmullen)
Rathmullen Yeomanry 23
Regiments
  62nd Foot 11
  79th Foot 23
  Royal Air Force 96, 98, 99
  82 Group 99
  245 Fighter Squadron 94, 95
  502 (Ulster) (Bomber) Sqn RAuxAF 83
  920 Sqn 93
  968 Sqn 93
  Royal Artillery 17, 19, 23, 37, 42, 51, 52, 55, 78, 84, 89, 103
  Royal Engineers 17, 18, 19, 22, 31, 45, 51, 55, 83, 84, 89
  Royal Garrison Artillery (RGA) 75
  Royal Irish Constabulary (RIC) 77
  Royal Navy 7, 12, 13, 15, 23, 40, 42, 45, 48, 53, 54, 56, 57,
    64, *70*, 73, 74, 75, 83, 85, 86, 88, 89, 90, 91, 93, 96, 98

Formations
1st Battle Sqn 70
3rd Battle Sqn 70
4th Battle Sqn 70
6th Battle Sqn 70
1st Light Cruiser Sqn 70
2nd Destroyer Flotilla 73
3rd Destroyer Flotilla 73
North Sea Hydrophone Flotilla 73
North Channel Patrol 73
Ships
Audacious 71, *71*
Benbow 53
Black Prince 45
Collingwood 54
Devastation 53, 54
Donegal 15
Doris 15
Dreadnought 54
Furious 94
King Edward VII 70
Magnamime 15
Robust 15
Thunderer 54
Warrior 45, *46*
Royal Ulster Constabulary 80

Saltpan Hill 21, 22, 23, 27
Shearer, Lt Col EDR, RA, TA 103
Sinn Féin 76
Smith, Capt Sir William 18, *18*, 20, 21, *21*, 24, *24*, 25, *25*, 26,
    27, 30, 34, *40*, 41
Strangford Lough 7, 49

Tandy, Napper 14, 15
Tarrant, Lt Col Charles 23, *24*
Thomson Graving Dock 73
Thurot, Adm 11, 12, 23
Tone, Wolfe 12, 13, 15
Tryon, Rear Adm Sir George, RN 57
Twiss, Col William, RE 22, 25

Ulster Home Guard 98, 99

Ulster Special Constabulary 77, 80

Ulster Volunteer Force 68, 69

United Irishmen 12, 13, 14, 20

US Army

Corps

XVth Corps 99

Divisions

1st Armoured 96

2nd Infantry 99

5th Infantry 99

8th Infantry 99

34th Infantry 96

82nd Airborne 99

Regiments

209th Coast Artillery (AA) 96

United States Army Air Force 41, 98

Victoria Barracks 86

Victoria Channel 68, 73

Warren, Commodore Sir John, RN 15

West Twin Island 68, 73, 83

Whiddy Island 20

Whitehead 75, 97, 99

Whitshed, Rear Adm, RN 39, 41

Whitworth, Joseph 47, 48

Wolseley, Lord 55

Yellow Ford, Battle of 10